# PUB WAI
## — IN —
# Nottinghamshire

# P U B   W A L K S
## — I N —
# Nottinghamshire

THIRTY CIRCULAR WALKS
AROUND NOTTINGHAMSHIRE INNS

## Peter Fooks

COUNTRYSIDE BOOKS
NEWBURY, BERKSHIRE

COUNTRYSIDE BOOKS
3 Catherine Road
Newbury, Berkshire

ISBN 1 85306 244 8

Designed by Mon Mohan
Cover illustration by Colin Doggett
Photographs and maps by the Author


Produced through MRM Associates Ltd., Reading
Typeset by Paragon Typesetters, Queensferry, Clwyd
Printed in England

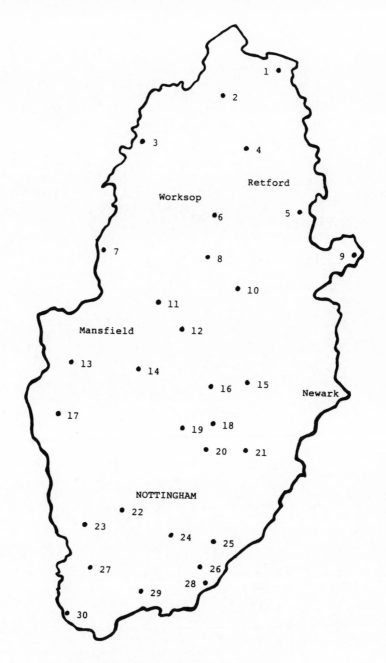

Area map showing locations of the walks.

# Mapping Symbols

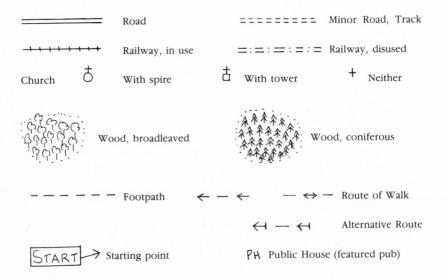

| | |
|---|---|
| ——————— Road | = = = = = = = = = Minor Road, Track |
| —+—+—+—+—+—+ Railway, in use | =:=:=:=:= Railway, disused |
| Church ☨ With spire | ☖ With tower  ✝ Neither |
| Wood, broadleaved | Wood, coniferous |
| – – – – – – Footpath | ← — ←  — ↔ — Route of Walk |
| | ⊢← — ←⊣ Alternative Route |
| START—→ Starting point | PH Public House (featured pub) |

# Contents

## Publisher's Note

We hope that you obtain considerable enjoyment from this book; great care has been taken in its preparation. However, changes of landlord and actual closures are sadly not uncommon. We are anxious that all details concerning both pubs and walks are kept as up to date as possible, and would therefore welcome information from readers which would be relevant to future editions.

# Introduction

Nottinghamshire is grossly underrated as a walking area, suffering for its close proximity to the more popular limestone and grit areas of the Peak District. I myself am not entirely guiltless in this respect, because I also have tended, over many years, to concentrate my walking activities rather more in Derbyshire than in my home county. The preparation of this book has served as a salutary – and long overdue – reminder to me of all that Nottinghamshire has to offer the wayfarer; its gentle rolling hills, ancient woodlands, rivers and canals, becks and dumbles.

Much of the survey work has been – quite rightly – a joint operation with my wife. All the inns have been sampled by one or both of us and have come up to expectations, providing perfect food, drink, service and company. A few years ago I served a term as a part-time barman. The sum total of pub grub at that time was roasted peanuts, potato crisps and cheese butties. Pub catering has improved beyond recognition since then – although my waistline hasn't!

Most of the inns will allow you to use their car parks while taking your walk, assuming you are giving them your custom, but it is sensible to ask permission; similarly if you want to eat your own sandwiches in the garden area. We have noticed, too, that most pubs have good lounge carpets. It is not good manners to barge in in muddy boots without first offering to remove them. In fact, all the walks, as described, start and finish at the featured inn, so it is no hardship, if you come by car, to change out of your boots before entering – or into them on leaving.

For those without transport of their own, we have provided basic information regarding transport services to the featured locations. These should not be accepted as complete – or, necessarily, accurate. Many local bus services, for instance, do not operate on Sundays. You are advised to check availability, and timings, with the various operators before setting out, or to ring the Buses Hotline on Nottingham (0602) 240000.

Something else that has changed a lot, for the better, in recent years, is the condition and usage of our county's rights of way. When I was a boy, waymarking was virtually non-existent, and you had to be a competent map-reader (and, as often as not, skilled in jungle warfare) to follow the footpaths. Things are much easier today and, by and large, the paths are well marked and easy to follow. All the routes described here are along definitive rights of way – or, if not so, on ways where the public clearly enjoy regular and unhindered usage.

The sketch maps provided are for guidance only and should not be regarded as infallible. We have provided details of the appropriate Landranger and Pathfinder maps, and you are recommended to use these, where possible, in association with the route instructions, bearing in mind, however, that there may be instances on these routes where footpaths have been legitimately diverted.

Generally speaking, boots are not obligatory in Nottinghamshire, but stout footwear – whether boots or shoes does not matter – is advisable. We do not have any mountains. But we do have farmyards and arable land, and some of our fields and lanes can be extremely wet and muddy, particularly in winter, after ploughing. It is also wise to carry rainwear, and spare woollens, even when the weather appears to be set fair.

One final point – it is worth remembering that the land is somebody's workshop, and most of us are there only as visitors. Courtesy costs nowt!

To the world in general, Nottinghamshire is the county of Robin Hood and D.H. Lawrence, of coal mines and power stations, of Trent Bridge and Nottingham Forest. But there is far more to our county than this – and it is hoped that, in following the walks described here, and in sampling the delights of some of our excellent hostelries (and our first-class breweries!), the reader will experience something of the pleasure and satisfaction that I have derived from my research and exploration.

Peter Fooks
Edwalton
Summer 1993

# Misterton
## The Packet

'An Everyday Pub for Country Folk' is the landlord's description of this homely canalside freehouse. The inn, the oldest part of which dates back to 1712, takes its name from the packet boats that used to transport grain along the canal for distribution around the countryside, as the horses used were stabled here. Tucked away out of the mainstream of village life, the Packet provides good food and drink and hospitable service, and is justly popular on that account. The colourful narrow boats, together with the ducks, on the Chesterfield Canal, add an additional lively touch to the charming setting.

Meals and bar snacks are available daily and evenings, except Mondays, with traditional Sunday lunches, and medieval banquets in the 18th century function room. A speciality of the house is its prime quality steaks, and you will also find a variety of fish and game dishes, as well as a selection of grills, snacks and sandwiches. Real ales include John Smith's Bitters, and a range of lagers are on sale here as well as both Strongbow and Woodpecker Cider on draught.

The inn has a no-smoking area and a family room, as well as an outside children's area and beer garden, and there is no objection to

11

patrons consuming their own food outside on non-catering days. Well behaved dogs are also welcome here.

Telephone: Gainsborough (0427) 890559.

*How to get there:* Misterton is on the A161 road between Beckingham and Haxey. The inn is at the eastern end of the village and on the northern bank of the Chesterfield Canal. Leave the main road immediately to the west of the railway bridge, cross the canal, and the inn will be found on your right.

*Parking:* In the inn's own car park.

*Public transport:* There are buses from Gainsborough and Retford (East Midland, Lincolnshire) and Doncaster (Lincolnshire).

*Length of the walk:* 4¼ miles. Maps: OS Landranger series 112 Scunthorpe, Pathfinder series SK 69/79 Harworth and Gringley on the Hill (GR SK 776947).

*The Idle is one of Nottinghamshire's lesser-known rivers, and the name is appropriate. For this is a walk for the idler, who wishes nothing better than a leisurely stroll along quiet and level waterside ways.*

**The Walk**
Follow the minor road west from the inn to join the main road through the town. Keep to the main road all the way onto the High Street and to the town centre. There is a footpath on the right, on the bend just beyond the Methodist chapel, but this is not recommended. Keep instead to the main road, turning right by the church, onto Haxey Road.

Leave Haxey Road by a waymarked path on the right, signposted for 'Misterton Soss and West Stockwith'. On reaching a field, turn left, crossing the next stile and immediately turning right and following the hedge. Turn right at the next fingerpost, then left again around the field to join a clear field path leading all the way to Misterton Soss, ignoring a farm track leading down to the buildings away to your right.

Cross the railway line, with great care as it is still in use. Take care also as you ascend and descend the greasy wooden steps on either side. Continue on over the field beyond to reach Soss Lane, and turn left.

Follow the lane round to a cottage and cross the footbridge over the river Idle. Turn right and follow the footpath along the top of the floodbank, gay, here, in spring, with snowdrops. Pass the floodgates,

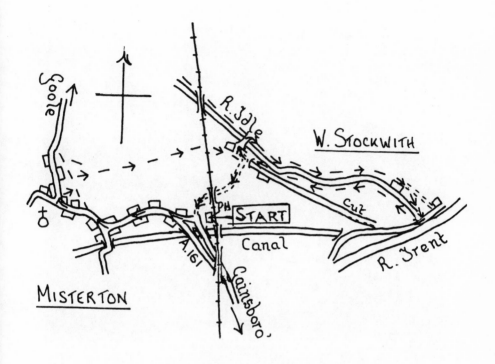

skirting around the buildings to rejoin the floodbank through to West Stockwith and the tidal river Trent. Cross the bridge and turn back along the southern bank of the Idle, again using the floodbank path. As you approach Misterton Soss, with its ancient mill buildings, you will note that the path passes between two separate waterways, the river on your right, and a cut on the left.

Beyond the buildings turn left onto Soss Lane. Ignore the path on your right by the kennels (the sharp-eyed will recognise this as the route by which we arrived earlier from Misterton), and continue straight ahead along the lane, all the way through to Misterton. On reaching the lane end, by the canal bridge, turn left for the inn.

# 2 Everton
## The Blacksmith's Arms

A freehouse, the Blacksmith's is about 300 years old, and started life, as the name suggests, as a smithy. The host is anxious to maintain the house as a traditional old-world pub, and the ancient timbers, low oak beams and homely atmosphere contribute in no small measure toward this end. I am assured that one particularly solid oak beam, beneath which you need to duck in passing between the bar and the lounge, started out as an acorn in Sherwood Forest, graduating to form the crossbeam of a sailing ship, before returning to home ground here in North Notts. To add a touch of authenticity to the tale, a ship's wheel, boat clock and a pair of brass pistols fill a place in the decor. A particularly pleasing feature, in winter, is the welcoming open coal fire in the little tile-floored bar room.

Real ales here include Younger Scotch Bitter, Theakston Best, Old Peculier, XB and Home Brewery Bitter, as well as a weekly guest beer. Strongbow Cider is available on draught. Bar meals are available every day, and in the evenings from Monday to Saturday. There is an extensive menu, including vegetarian dishes and children's specials, and a traditional roast for Sunday lunch. But the speciality of the house is the crêperie, with a staggering selection of savoury, sweet and 'special' versions to choose from.

The Blacksmith's has a beer garden, as well as a family room and a garden area for the children, if accompanied by their parents. There is no objection to patrons eating their own food in the garden area, outside catering hours.

Telephone: Retford (0777) 817281.

*How to get there:* Everton lies on the A631 Bawtry to Gainsborough road, about 3½ miles east of Bawtry. The inn is reached from Chapel Lane, which leaves the main road at the western end of the village, and is well advertised.

*Parking:* The Blacksmith's has its own extensive car park for patrons – but do ask if you want to leave your car there for the duration of your walk. On-street parking is not too difficult, particularly in the vicinity of the parish church.

*Public transport:* Buses run from Retford and Bawtry (various operators), Gainsborough and Worksop (East Midland and

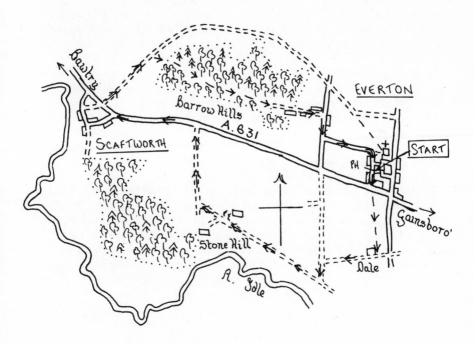

Lincolnshire Road Car), Doncaster and Sheffield (Lincolnshire Road Car).

*Length of the walk:* 5 miles. Maps: OS Landranger series 111 Sheffield and Doncaster, Pathfinder series SK 69/79 Harworth and Gringley on the Hill (GR SK 691912).

*Everton is one of Nottinghamshire's most northerly villages and is a pretty place of pleasant red-brick cottages and friendly people, with a charming pub. This is an easy stroll, culminating in a delightful walk over the wooded Barrow Hills.*

## The Walk
Leaving the inn, follow Ferry Lane away from the Green to reach Chapel Lane and turn left, following the lane down to the main road. Cross a stile directly opposite and follow a footpath by the fieldside all the way through to a track, Broomhill Lane. Turn right, passing a cottage (The Dale) and following the track on to a T junction.

Turn left and, at a second T junction, right again, now following Youldholes Lane. After passing a pair of derelict cottages (Stone Hill Cottages), the track goes left towards Stone Hill Farm, but keep straight ahead here, following a green track to another T junction. Turn right, following a good track down to the road, resisting the temptation on the way to turn left onto an enticing green lane – it leads nowhere!

Go left and follow the road to the outskirts of Scaftworth. This little village is not on our route, but it offers a pleasant diversion, particularly if you are thirsty and wish to take ale at the King William. Otherwise, turn right and follow Theaker Lane, a good clear broad track which, with its successor (Pasture Lane), circles around the Barrow Hills to reach Everton. At the end of the hard surface turn right, following a footpath up to the woods.

There are several variations to the route through the woods, all very inviting to the adventurous explorer. The main track branches shortly after entering the wood. Take the right hand path, climbing steeply through mixed woodland to reach the highest parts of the wood, before emerging onto a minor road leading down into the hamlet of Harwell. Turn right along the village street, passing Mansfield Farm and bearing left along a narrow side lane to reach Chapel Lane, and Everton village.

# ③ Carlton in Lindrick
## The Blue Bell

Built about 300 years ago, the stone-built Blue Bell retains the charm and atmosphere of a typical village inn. The attractive outward aspect is matched by the clean and welcoming neatness of the cosy lounge, with its period pictures of village scenes and traditional rural crafts. A freehouse, you will find a selection of real ales here, including Stones, Theakston and Tetley Bitter, as well as Strongbow and Woodpecker Cider on draught.

Bar snacks are available Monday to Saturday between 12 noon and 2 pm, and include a wide selection of sandwiches, Yorkshire pudding dishes and jacket potatoes. My own personal recommendation is the scrumptious home-made pie and peas. You can top out with either coffee or tea. Snacks are not provided on Sundays, but a traditional Sunday lunch is, and the lounge is often busy on these days.

There is a combined beer garden and play area, and patrons are welcome to eat their own food there when meals are not available. Well behaved dogs are welcome but not, please, in the lounge.

Telephone: Worksop (0909) 730291.

*How to get there:* Carlton in Lindrick bestrides the main A60 road, about 3½ miles north of Worksop. The Blue Bell is in the centre of

the village, on the eastern side of the road.

*Parking:* There is adequate parking at the inn, and you are welcome to leave your transport there while you take your walk. If you are not using the inn's facilities, you will find a useful parking space (and the opportunity to shorten the walk a little), on Church Lane, opposite the parish church.

*Public transport:* A frequent bus service (East Midland) from Worksop and Doncaster calls here.

*Length of the walk:* 3½ miles. Maps: OS Landranger series 120 Mansfield and the Dukeries, Pathfinder series SK 48/58 Aughton and Carlton in Lindrick (GR SK 592845).

*Carlton in Lindrick is close to the South Yorkshire border, and there is something of Yorkshire in the atmosphere here, with a preponderence of stone in the traditional buildings. The main road runs through the centre of the village, but the old road curves around on either side, taking the explorer to quieter, more rural vistas. And that is the way we set out.*

## The Walk

Cross the road from the inn and walk south, turning off along Church Lane. Pass the church and continue as far as the old mill, crossing the stream. Over the stream, leave the road, bearing right along a lesser way, and immediately enter a waymarked bridleway between the buildings on your left.

On reaching the fields, the path branches. Take the rightward branch and cross two fields, making directly for a cottage. Emerge on the road and turn right, passing the cottage. On the bend leave the road, walking straight ahead on a pleasant green track and heading for Holme House Farm.

Follow the lane past the farm, continuing on ahead along a farm track to the left of a pair of bungalows. On reaching a T junction turn right, descending easily. At a 'Private Road' sign leave the track, bearing left onto a waymarked bridleway to cross a stream, then on in the direction of Wallingwells, visible ahead over the fields. At an intersecting path turn right, passing to the left of a small group of modern homes, and continuing straight ahead. In the farthest field bear left, to reach Carlton Wood.

Follow a clear path through the wood. There are a number of alternative routes and it does not matter a lot which of these you choose to follow – unless you are a hopeless navigator they will all lead either to the church or the High Road. The most direct route to the church, if that is where you are parked, is via the clear main path, deviating neither to left nor to right. If you are making for the Blue Bell, follow this same path until you reach an equally distinct path branching off left, which will lead you, with fields now visible through the trees on your right, to the edge of a housing estate. Follow the path along the edge of the wood, emerging into an enclosed footpath with fields on your right and houses on the left, to arrive at the High Road, almost opposite the inn.

# **Hayton**
## The Boat Inn

Set in pleasant rural surroundings on the banks of the tranquil Chesterfield Canal, and only three miles from the busy market town of Retford, the Boat is a deservedly popular freehouse and an excellent place to pause for refreshment. Linger longer if the fancy takes you, for accommodation is available and the less energetic can spend a pleasant break by the canalside, fishing, or simply watching the world go by. If you come in winter, an open coal fire in the bar area guarantees a cosy welcome.

Ales on offer include hand-pulled bitters, particularly Bass, Stones and Boddingtons, and there is draught cider too. A wide range of bar snacks and meals is available daily, and evenings too, from Sunday through to Saturday, and there is a separate restaurant area for those who prefer a more formal meal. Whether your taste is for a simple snack or a full meal, you are sure to find satisfaction here, the range is so comprehensive as to be breathtaking. I settled for hot roast pork and stuffing, with French bread, chips and salad – just try getting your teeth into that lot for a snack!

There is a beer garden and well-equipped children's play area, as well as a family room. Customers may eat their own snap in the garden area on those rare occasions when food is not available. Well behaved dogs are welcome.

Telephone: Retford (0777) 700158.

*How to get there:* Leave the A620 Retford to Gainsborough road at Clarborough, joining the B1403 at the southern end of Hayton village. Follow the road through the village and the Boat Inn is at the very end, immediately before the canal bridge.

*Parking:* Available in the pub car park.

*Public transport:* Buses run from Retford and Gainsborough (Retford and District, Lincolnshire Road Car, East Midland).

*Length of the walk:* 4 miles. Maps: OS Landranger series 120 Mansfield and the Dukeries, Pathfinder series SK 68/78 East Retford North, and Blyth (GR SK 728852).

*The villages of Hayton and Clarborough are so close as to form a single linear community bestriding the A620 and B1403 roads and lying parallel to the Chesterfield Canal, yet each retains its own distinctive identity. This walk encircles, rather than visits, both villages, following first the peaceful canal towpath, then crossing over to return via the eastern hillside. A splendid walk, culminating in gloriously wide views over three counties.*

**The Walk**

From the inn, cross the bridge (and the road) and descend to the canalside, passing under the bridge to follow the grassy towpath in a southerly direction. A pleasant waterside ramble follows, passing under several attractive original canal bridges, and affording excellent views of Hayton parish church, across the meadows on the opposite bank.

On reaching a road (the Gate Inn is opposite), ascend to and cross the bridge. Take a footpath immediately on the right. Keep to the canal bank for a short distance, passing the Gill Green Walk metalled path, then bearing left just before a canalside bench to reach a stile. Cross a field path to reach a housing estate, turning left into South View Drive and following this road and the subsequent bridle/footway (Little Lane) beside a stream to reach the A620 road.

Cross the road and go along Howbeck Lane. At the end of the houses take a footpath on the left, crossing several fields to remeet the A620. Cross over and continue along an enclosed green lane (Lovers' Walk), waymarked as a public bridleway. At a crossways turn right, following Hangingside Lane uphill, and swinging left with the track as

21

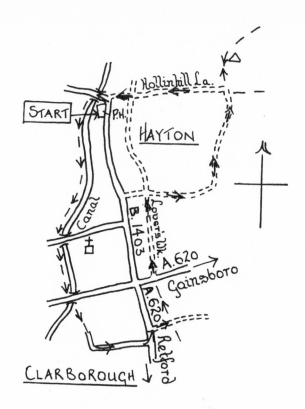

the massive structure of West Burton Power Station comes into view ahead.

Go across Hollinhill Lane. The direct route back to the Boat Inn follows this track, but anyone taking the direct route at this stage will be denying him/herself a splendid view. Continue ahead on the field path to reach the summit of the hill, marked by a trig point. The pillar is a few yards off the path but, provided you use your commonsense and keep to the field edge, you are unlikely to be challenged. The views from this modest summit (223 ft) are wide and impressive. On a clear day, Lincoln Cathedral will be visible 17 miles away to the east. West Burton Power Station steals the scene, but the distant views over the plains and fenlands of North Notts, Lincolnshire, and South Yorkshire, make the short extension (300 yards) from Hollinhill Lane well worth while.

Return now to Hollinhill Lane and descend by this pleasant track to Townend Bridge, and the Boat Inn.

# Laneham
## The Butcher's Arms

The village of Laneham is surprisingly secluded and tranquil, despite the close proximity of the busy A57 trunk road to the south, and the overbearing presence to the north of Cottam Power Station. It is really two villages, Church Laneham, the smaller hamlet beside the river, and Laneham proper, half a mile to the west. It is here, in the centre of the village, that you will find the Butcher's Arms, a 400 year old, prominent white-painted village inn, combining the very best of traditional values and modern requirements.

The cosy and welcoming lounge bar features a beautiful inglenook fireplace and the familiar low beams. Stuffed owls, kingfishers and red squirrels add an interesting touch, along with various items of brass and copperware, and an ingeniously adapted beam scale on the bar counter makes an unusual floral feature. The public bar, meanwhile, has been modernised with the addition of a conservatory extension, to include a pool table, while an adjacent gym and health studio adds that unique extra something to this welcoming freehouse.

Meals and bar snacks are obtainable at lunchtime and in the evening, seven days a week. If a light snack is all you require, you might settle for an omelette, or a baked potato or choose from a variety of main

23

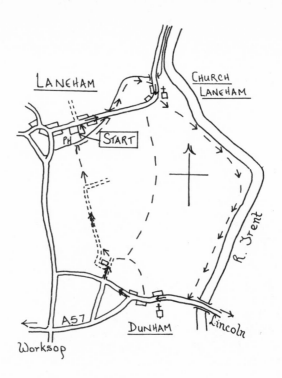

courses, including fish, chicken, lasagne, steak and kidney pie or cottage pie. For the more ambitious, there is also a choice of starters, such as prawn and cucumber cocktail, squid in butter, and longboat potato shells, with a choice of sweets, and coffee – not forgetting a comprehensive wine list. Real ales include Boddingtons, Marston's Pedigree, and guest ales, and the speciality in draught cider here is Autumn Gold.

The Butcher's Arms has a beer garden and kiddies' playground outside. Dogs are welcome as long as they stay well away from the eating areas.

Telephone: Retford (0777) 228255.

*How to get there:* From the A57 Lincoln to Worksop road turn north at the western end of Dunham on Trent, following the Laneham and Cottam road. Turn off a good mile out of Dunham to reach Laneham village, turning right at the road junction onto Main Street to reach the inn.

*Parking:* You may leave your vehicle in the inn car park while you take your walk.

24

*Public transport:* Buses come here from Retford (Retford District, Lincolnshire, East Midland) and Tuxford (Retford District).

*Length of the walk:* 4½ miles. Maps: OS Landranger series 121 Lincoln and surrounding areas, Pathfinder series SK 87/97 Lincoln and Saxilby (GR SK 804762).

*For much of its length the river Trent forms the boundary between Nottinghamshire and Lincolnshire; and one of the few road crossings between the two is the toll bridge at Dunham. We walk first to the tiny riverside hamlet of Church Laneham with its ancient parish church and, in season, its complement of speed boats, water skiers and picnickers. We then follow the peaceful riverside footpath to Dunham Bridge, returning by easy level field paths to Laneham village.*

**The Walk**
Turn right from the inn, following the main street in the direction of Church Laneham. Cross the floodbank and a stream and turn left, following a footpath (waymarked as the Trent Valley Way) along the top of this second floodbank. On reaching the lock gates, bear right to a toilet block and follow the metalled footpath down to the road.

Turn right along the road and pass through the church gates. The church is worth visiting and has an ancient door – said to be eight hundred years old and one of the oldest in England. There is also a beautiful half-timbered porch, which looks extremely old, but which in reality was constructed in the 20th century.

Bear right through the churchyard to a stile and go alongside the ensuing fence to the floodbank, which is followed all the way to Dunham and the toll bridge. Continue on the road through Dunham village, turning right onto the Laneham road by the White Swan. Just past the next junction (Upper Row), turn right by a row of cottages. Keep straight ahead on a farm track, bearing left after the final house to reach a metal farm gate. Follow the hedge across the next field, swinging right onto a farm lane.

The track, Chequers Lane, now runs straight ahead, and Laneham is visible in front across these vast open acres. Directly underneath a power line, the track turns sharp right. Continue ahead here, following the right hand side of the ditch. At the end of the field cross a stile and continue for a short distance to reach the floodbank and here turn right. Pass by a farm bridge and continue on to reach a second (foot) bridge. Go over this and bear left to cross a stile. Follow an enclosed path beside the hedge through to Laneham village, and turn left back to the inn.

# ⑥ Elkesley
# The Robin Hood

No Pub Walks guide to Nottinghamshire would be complete without at least one hostelry dedicated to the county's most celebrated legendary hero; and where better to find such an inn than here in the heart of Sherwood Forest? A very busy and popular watering hole, the Robin Hood's clientele extends far beyond the confines of this secluded little village, and the inn owes its success largely to a reputation for good food and fine ales, built up by the landlord and staff, not only with the locals, but also with visitors from the neighbouring towns, and escapees from the adjacent busy A1 trunk road.

Although outwardly displaying no indications of great age, parts of the building are claimed to date from the 15th and 16th centuries, but the interior is pleasantly modern, without flashiness.

One of Whitbread's houses, the Robin Hood offers Boddingtons, Castle Eden and Trophy real ales, as well as Strongbow Cider on draught – appropriate for the archers among us!

Food is available at lunchtimes, seven days a week, and in the evenings from Monday to Saturday, and the landlord is the chef. If you want to dine in character you will order the Robin Hood mixed grill, or you may choose from a selection of chicken, trout or steak dishes.

Then there are various sandwiches, rolls, snacks and salads, and a full wine list – not to mention waitress service in the separate dining area. The inn has a beer garden/play area – and children are allowed inside, when dining. Well behaved dogs are welcome, but in the public bar only.

Telephone: Retford (0777) 838259.

*How to get there:* From the south side of the A1 Newark to Doncaster road, turn off between the Markham and Clumber roundabouts.

*Parking:* Parking is available at the inn.

*Public transport:* There are buses from Nottingham, Retford and Worksop (East Midland), Retford, New Ollerton, Nottingham, Tuxford and Newark (Retford and District), and Retford, Tuxford and Newark (Kettlewell).

*Length of the walk:* 5¼ miles. Maps: OS Landranger series 120 Mansfield and the Dukeries, Pathfinder series SK 67/77 Clumber Park (GR SK 690755).

*Sherwood Forest and the Dukeries – the great estates of Clumber, Thoresby, Welbeck and Rufford – are synonymous, much of the ancient forest areas having been assimilated into the ducal estates. This walk is over lands which form an integral part of the Clumber estates, but are outside the popular honeypot of Clumber Park itself. In the course of our journey we twice cross the lively little river Poulter which, before reaching here, has already fed the estate lakes of Welbeck and Clumber; we also cross, again twice, the long, straight West Drayton Avenue, originally provided as a driveway to Clumber. And we visit the neighbouring prize-winning village of Bothamsall, with its ancient castle mound.*

**The Walk**
Follow the High Street past the church and on along the succeeding lane (Coalpit Lane). After passing a council estate continue past three fields before turning left along a metalled farm lane. Pass a bungalow and reach a T junction, turning right and continuing beneath a telephone line. At a farm entrance bear right and follow a footpath through to a metalled farm access road, turning right and then, with the road, left.

At the next bend turn left, by a brick pillar, onto a rough track and cross the river Poulter by a footbridge beside a ford – watch out for gaps in the planks of the bridge! Continue through woodland, and a pleasant clearing, then keep straight ahead to pass the first turning on the left and arrive at a private entrance gate. Turn left. Follow the path

beneath telegraph wires. On reaching the fields keep straight on, still beneath the wires, to cross West Drayton Avenue and on along a rough track. At the top of the hill, pass a reservoir and turn left along the nearside wall of a barn, following the hedge and making for a distant wooded knoll. In the third field, bear slightly left of the knoll to reach the road – and a welcome seat.

Before continuing, you may like to visit the motte – for that is what the knoll is. Its posh name is Bothamsall Castle, and access is recommended – because it's there, and to admire the view. But be sure to close the gate behind you when entering and leaving.

From the gateway, follow the road into Bothamsall, where a plate by the church gate tells us that this was the winner of a Best Kept Village award in 1986, 1987 and 1988. It is still a neat and pretty place.

Follow the side road to the left of the church, past a windpump and on along the ensuing green lane/farm track to Haughton Park House

Farm – admire the fine farmhouse building. As you approach the farm, you will no doubt observe the towers of Bevercotes Colliery showing their heads above the woods ahead.

Turn left with the track and recross West Drayton Avenue, continuing on ahead and bearing left into the woods as you pass Beggar's Rest Cottage. Follow the route as directed by the blue arrows through the woods, ignoring all other turnings. Recross the river Poulter and continue uphill by the fence. On reaching a trackway bear left a little to continue, still in the same direction, on the left side of the hedge. Turn right with the path to reach the sports ground, passing around two sides of the field to reach the entrance drive and the High Street.

# ⑦ Nether Langwith
## The Jug and Glass

There can be few more perfect situations for a typical English country pub than that of the Jug and Glass. Set back from the main Bolsover to Cuckney road and overlooking the charming little river Poulter with its waterfowl and playing children, this delightful 300 year old former coaching inn is hidden from sight to the motorist approaching from the east, right up to the very last moment, when it springs into view with breathtaking suddenness. This inn has no beer garden, because it has no need of one, possessing a much more desirable facility in its beautiful riverside frontage, with picnic tables, and grassland aplenty.

The internal arrangements of this welcoming Hardys and Hansons house are every bit as attractive as the external, with brasses, milk dippers, chinaware and an immense vase of 'Ali Baba' jar proportions, as well as an open fireplace. There is also a particularly appealing group of Victorian-style pictures of children at play – the familiar games of whip and top, conkers, and 'Rum-stick-a-bum'.

Real ales here include Kimberley Classic and Kimberley Bitter, and both Strongbow and Autumn Gold Cider are available on draught. Bar snacks are served at lunchtime, and there are evening meals too, from

Monday to Saturday. The bill of fare is impressive, with a wide selection of fish, meat and chicken dishes, pizzas, salads, snacks and sandwiches, not to mention giant Yorkshire puddings and a truly tempting cottage pie. If your visit is on a Sunday, you can have a traditional Sunday dinner. Children are catered for with their own special menu. Dogs, if well behaved, are welcome in the non-food areas.

Telephone: Mansfield (0623) 742283.

*How to get there:* From Cuckney, which, although tiny, stands on the junction of main roads from Sheffield, Worksop, Mansfield, Ollerton and Bolsover, take the A632 towards Bolsover. The Jug and Glass is in an unmissable position, overlooking the main road through Nether Langwith from across the river Poulter.

*Parking:* The inn has two car parks of its own, either of which you may use while taking your stroll.

*Public transport:* Mansfield District buses from Mansfield and Worksop stop in the village.

*Length of the walk:* 4 miles. Maps: OS Landranger series 120 Mansfield and the Dukeries, Pathfinder series SK 46/56 Mansfield North and SK 47/57 Staveley (GR SK 534704).

*There are two Langwiths – Upper Langwith, the larger, industrial Derbyshire town, and Nether Langwith, its smaller, more residential, Nottinghamshire counterpart, cheek by jowl with traditional coal mining areas. Throughout the walk you will come across evidence of the mines, surrounded by the attractive fields and woods of the area, which also provide a flavour of the nearby Dukeries estates (the four ducal estates that take up practically the whole of Sherwood Forest).*

**The Walk**
Leaving the inn, cross the road and follow the lane immediately opposite, between holly hedges, all the way through to Boon Hills Wood. On entering the wood bear right, following a clear woodland path close inside the woodland edge. This path is not marked on the map but the evidence on the ground plainly indicates its regular and popular use. Where the path forks, bear left, climbing out of the wood to join a farm track and turn right. Continue along the ensuing path, with a stone wall on your left and the woods on your right. At the end of the wood, turn left at a T junction and follow the broad track to New Plantation.

The OS map shows the route from here as following a path through

31

the wood from the point where the track meets a railway line. In practice, this path turns out to be impossibly wet underfoot, and here, once again, popular custom and commonsense dictate an easier route. Turn left on reaching New Plantation and follow a well defined track around two sides of the wood. Near the end of the wood, on its second side, bear left across more open ground to arrive at a disused mineral railway.

Descend by steps to the trackbed. A pair of derelict and rusty cars here do nothing to enhance the view – but so long as they remain they serve as an infallible guide to the crossing point! Turn left in the bed (backs to the wrecks) and look carefully for a run of steps, rather overgrown and perhaps not readily visible, ascending to cross the fence on the right at the top of the cutting. Here again the condition of the stile suggests that the path is not heavily used, but crossing presents no great difficulty.

Bear left over the stile, crossing a largish field and aiming to the left of a group (or so it appears on first sight) of three trees – in practice, they are nowhere near each other. This field was uncultivated when we came, and the keening of lapwings suggested the possible presence of nests, so look where you are putting your feet!

Over the field pass through a snicket (a gap between two posts) in the fence and cross the next field directly. Across this field turn right and continue beside the wood (Lord Stubbins Wood) to a turning left, and then follow the delightful woodland path through to the far side. Turn right in the field, following the edge of the wood over two fields, then through a gap on the right at the end of the wood, and left again through a farm gateway, to follow the track round and down beside the fields, passing through a Model Flyers' Club site to reach William Wood Lane.

Turn left and follow the lane through to the old mineral railway. The landfill site to the right of the lane may be thought rather unsightly – but it is all in a good cause. The Warsop Colliery tip area is being reclaimed, and the evidence of those parts which have already been landscaped suggests an excellent improvement in prospect.

Cross the old railway and turn left, following the edge of the field round and down, beneath the telephone wires, over three fields. At the end of the third field a superfluous long stile (or could it be a bench?) links two fields and a wood. As a stile it serves no useful purpose, because one can easily pass through without climbing over, but as a resting place, there is none better!

Turn left and follow the footpath through the woods and round, now keeping just inside the woods, to reach Top Farm. Cross the stile here and bear right, following the track back, by your outward route once more, to Nether Langwith.

# 8 Walesby
## The Carpenter's Arms

A notice outside the Carpenter's proclaims a welcome to scouts, campers and caravanners; a curious combination of pubgoers, it might be supposed, but not out of place here, for this attractive hostelry is as convenient to the popular Walesby Forest Scout Camp as it is to the village of Walesby. Walkers are not specified, but it goes without saying that these – and, indeed, all comers – find a genuine welcome here. This Everard's house – despite being situated on the 'wrong' side of the road for Walesby village – clearly has its own regular clientele of satisfied locals in addition to the casual callers, attracted by the bright and friendly look of the place.

The inn was built in the 19th century, so it is not the oldest in the county. All the same, it does boast the distinction of its own resident ghost, a lady wearing a white pinafore and a white poke bonnet.

You will find traditional ales here, both Everards and Adnams, as well as draught cider – Strongbow and Woodpecker. There is an impressive range of full meals and bar snacks on offer daily, and in the evenings too, and a speciality of the house is the 'Dukeries' potato, in a variety of guises – Thoresby, Clumber, Rufford and Welbeck – the range of fillings including chicken, mushrooms, garlic mayonnaise and

crabmeat. Outside there is a beer garden/children's play area, where customers are welcome to consume their own food outside catering hours.
Telephone: Mansfield (0623) 860716.

*How to get there:* From the A614 Nottingham/Doncaster road, turn off to the east 1½ miles north of the Ollerton roundabout, following the signposted road through to Walesby. If approaching via the A1, turn south between West Drayton and Elkesley, onto the B6387 Gamston/Boughton road. The inn stands on the edge of the village, on the corner of the Boughton road and Brake Road.

*Parking:* Customers are welcome to make use of the inn's own spacious car park.

*Public transport:* There are buses from Mansfield (East Midland), also from Retford, New Ollerton and Nottingham (Retford and District, and East Midland).

*Length of the walk:* 4¼ miles. Maps: OS Landranger series 120 Mansfield and the Dukeries, Pathfinder series SK 66/76 Ollerton and SK 67/77 Clumber Park and East Markham (GR SK 680705).

*The camp site at Walesby Forest has been a mecca to members of the Scout movement for more than half a century, and it is appropriate that, while respecting the privacy of the tented areas, our walk should pass around the perimeter of this delightful reserve of pine woods and sandlands. For some of the way we follow the course of the meandering river Maun, before returning to Walesby by the forestry plantation of Boughton Brake.*

**The Walk**
Follow the road north from the inn, passing the drive of Furze Court on your left and taking the next turning (Forest Lane), also on the left. Beyond a farm gate, a poultry farm is passed and a bridge over a mineral line crossed, after which the way continues as a green lane. Beyond a second farm gate the track reverts to an enclosed footpath, following the perimeter of the Scout Camp. Principally for boys from the city and county of Nottingham, the camp site here has entertained visitors from throughout Great Britain and, indeed, the world. My own first visit took place in the spring of 1945 and in the ensuing years I developed a particular affection for this site.
At a bend in the path turn right, continuing northwards between the campsite and a private field. On reaching a wood bear left, to follow the path just within the woodland, and now in a westerly direction.

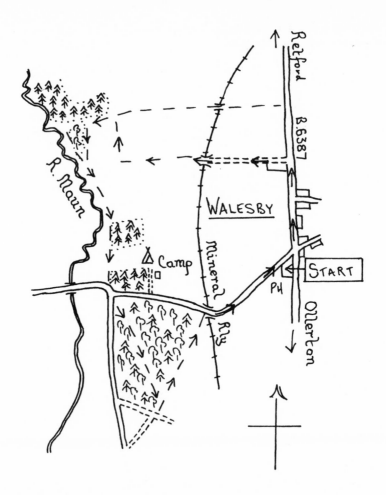

A track will be met crossing from left to right. The most direct route
to our destination of Chapel Wood follows this track to the left, but
you are recommended to simply bear left a little to continue beside
the wood, still going west, with a pine wood on your right and broad-
leaves (mainly birch) to your left. The path emerges onto more open
ground as it descends sharply towards the river Maun, now visible
ahead and below.

Bear left now along a narrow path, at first keeping well to the left
of the river, but gradually approaching nearer until you arrive at a low
sandstone clifftop overlooking the river, close to the same track you
crossed earlier. There used to be a little cave in the face of this cliff

with the grandiose title of Robin Hood's Cave. It may be there yet, if generations of adventurous small boys have not eroded it away, but whether it is worth seeking out is a matter of opinion! It was never very impressive in my time, and I could never conceive the situation in which the outlaw would have wished to insinuate his frame into its confined space.

Rejoin the main track and continue, passing to the right successively of Chapel Wood, the main camping field, and Whitewater Wood, to emerge onto Brake Road.

The road forms a dog-leg here, bending right then left again before continuing past Whitewater Wood. A second road leads off here, heading for New Ollerton and passing Boughton Brake. Enter the woodland of the Brake, following a footpath at an angle of about 45° to the road junction. Keep to the clear track ahead, ignoring all side turnings and intersections until buildings come into view ahead, and you emerge from the wood. Turn sharp left now, following a way-marked path in an approximately north easterly direction beside the wood. Continue alongside the wood until you reach Brake Road again, at the side of the mineral line. Turn right and follow the road back to the inn.

# Harby
## The Bottle and Glass

9

Harby is the most easterly village in Nottinghamshire, occupying a position no more than ½ mile from the Lincolnshire border. Tucked away from the rush and bustle of the county's more illustrious towns and villages, it nevertheless has its own place in the history books, for it was here that Queen Eleanor, the consort of Edward I, died in 1290, and began her solemn journey to Westminster Abbey.

A homely, family-run freehouse, the history of the Bottle and Glass dates back to the 17th century. The staff here are tremendously friendly and obliging, an attribute which is clearly reflected in the loyalty of its regular clientele, and which extends in equal measure to the casual visitor. The various bars and dining areas are grouped around a central counter area, and a striking feature of the lounge, in which we ate, is the attractive brick-built chimney breast and fireplace – with a cheerful coal fire in season.

Real ales at the Bottle and Glass include Youngers Scotch, No 3 and Adnams, with Strongbow Cider in the bottle and Scrumpy Jack on draught. Hot and cold food is available daily and in the evenings, and there are traditional Sunday lunches. The comprehensive menu includes a wide selection of pastas, curries, steaks, fish, salads and snacks, not to mention home-made pies, the king among which must surely be the Desperate Dan Cow Pie (without the horns, we suppose!). Vegetarians and children are also catered for. There is a combined children's area and beer garden, as well as a family dining area. Well behaved dogs are welcome, though not in the public eating areas.

Telephone: Lincoln (0522) 703438.

*How to get there:* Harby is reached from either the A1133 Newark/Gainsborough road, turning off on the signposted Harby road at Besthorpe, or the B1190 Saxilby/North Hykeham road, leaving at Five Lane Ends, one mile south of the A57 junction.

*Parking:* There is ample parking space at the inn, and you may leave your car here while you go walkabout.

*Public transport:* Buses run from Newark and Saxilby (Travel Wright).

*Length of the walk:* 6¾ miles. Maps: OS Landranger series 121 Lincoln, Pathfinder series SK 87/97 Lincoln and Saxilby (GR 880708). This walk is the longest in the collection, and spends as much time in Lincolnshire as it does in our home county; but we make no apology on either count. Only the explanation that, of the alternatives available, this is the most satisfying. However, if you are a purist, you can reduce the Lincolnshire content (and the total distance) by joining the road at Broadholme and following the tarmac, either on foot or by bus, back to Harby. But check the bus service first if you plan to use it!

*Our route crosses the trackbed of the former Lincoln to Mansfield railway after which, in the course of our journey, we cross the county boundary no fewer than four times, via arable fields and dikes, and crossing the vast Skellingthorpe Big Wood, before returning to Harby by our outward route.*

**The Walk**
Take the road northwards from the inn, turning right on the bend and following the waymarked farm lane. On reaching a dismantled railway, cross over, turning right in the field opposite and following the hedge for a short distance, before striking off left, passing to the right of a pylon, to reach the fence. Do not cross the fence, but turn left, following the edge of the field to merge with a farm track. At the end of a hedge turn right to reach and cross a stile, then go over two fields to arrive at Carr Lane (B1190).

Cross the road and take the clear path across the field ahead, passing to the right of Carr Farm, a modern farmhouse building. Turn left and

39

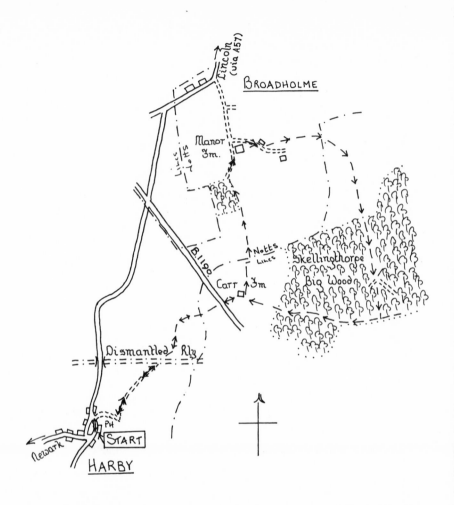

right through the farm gates, in dog-leg fashion, immediately turning left through the second gate and following the fence and succeeding hedge for the full length of the field. Continue right along the facing hedge to reach and cross a tricky stile and plank bridge. Bear right a little and follow the dike, crossing over at the bend to continue ahead on a field track to reach a wood (Broadholme Gorse). Follow a good track alongside the wood, bearing right at the end, and then left over a field to reach Manor Farm. Pass the farm on its left, then turn right along the waymarked metalled farm lane. Follow this as far as a house on the left, then turn left onto the waymarked bridleway.

Take the path around the edge of two fields, with a dike on your

40

left. In the third field bear right, making for the distant woods. Follow the clear and improving path – which, in its later stages, keeps to the highest ground – over vast acres, to reach and enter the woodland (Skellingthorpe Big Wood).

Continue ahead through the trees, following the waymarked bridleway. At a crossways, leave the wider track to continue straight ahead on the footpath. Ignore broader ways to right and left and pass to the rear of the bungalows. At the end of the woods, meet a T junction and turn right onto a waymarked bridleway, with a ditch on your left and the woods on your right.

Follow the woodland path, which tends to be very wet, through to a stile, and cross over to rejoin the fields. Bear slightly right over the first field to reach a pair of metal gates, then go along the track to reach Carr Farm, from where the way follows your outward route, over the road and across the former railway, back to Harby.

# ⑩ Laxton
## The Dovecote Inn

The Dovecote Inn has a special place in the life of Laxton, for it is here that the Court Leet meets to exercise its duties of administering the ancient 'open field' system of cultivation. Laxton is the last place in England where the medieval tradition survives, and the three field rotation of winter wheat, spring crops and fallow (or forage crop) is still followed to this day. The Dovecote is a deservedly popular, traditional village inn, a maze of little interconnecting rooms where the staff bustle to and fro attending to the inner needs of the customer. The traditional decor includes a selection of paintings by a local artist, M.E. Brunskill of Kirton, which the discerning customer is able to purchase.

A freehouse, you will nevertheless be able to drink Mansfield ales here, both Riding and Old Baily being on offer, as well as Bulmers Cider on draught. Food is available seven days a week, lunchtimes and evenings. The bill of fare is impressive, with a selection of salads, grills, meat dishes and sandwiches to tempt the palate. On Sunday you can opt for a full dinner of roast beef and Yorkshire pudding, and specials include sirloin steak, beef salad, ploughman's lunch, fisherman's pie and Japanese prawns. The children are not forgotten for they, too, have their own menu, as well as a play area outside. There is also a beer garden and a family room. Guide dogs only are allowed inside, for food hygiene reasons.

Customers are not encouraged to eat their own food on the premises – but then, with such a vast range of food on offer, it would perhaps be tactless to consider it!

Telephone: Retford (0777) 871586.

*How to get there:* From the Ollerton roundabout on the A614 Nottingham/Doncaster road, follow the A6075 through New Ollerton and Boughton, turning off about a mile further on, where the main road takes a sharp left turn for Kirton. Follow the side road from here, signposted for Laxton, under the railway bridge. Laxton is about 2 ½ to 3 miles along this road.

*Parking:* The Dovecote has its own car park, which patrons are welcome to use while taking their walk. But it might be more considerate to use the adjacent visitor centre car park, which is roomier.

*Public transport:* Buses run from Worksop, Retford and Nottingham (East Midland), as well as Tuxford and New Ollerton (Lincolnshire Road Car).

*Length of the walk:* 4 miles. Maps: OS Landranger series 120 Mansfield and the Dukeries, Pathfinder series SK 66/76 Ollerton (GR 724671).

*Our walk today takes us on a circuit of the west field, one of three participating in the traditional rotation of crops. We pass close by – with the option to visit – the site of Laxton Castle; a motte and bailey claimed to be the best preserved, and possibly the finest, in the county. And for good measure, you are recommended to call in, on returning to the inn, at the adjacent visitor centre.*

## The Walk

Bear right on leaving the car park, following the main street past the impressive 12th century parish church of St Michael. Towards the end of the village, bear right along a side lane. Where the metalled road ends, continue half left, following an enclosed green lane. This leads on to the west field.

Follow the hedge-side path and the succeeding green track, and, where the track bends right at a hedge, keep straight forward through the gap and by the side of the next field. Turn left with the hedge and then right again, crossing the open field and making for a white cottage, to reach the road, and a footpath sign.

43

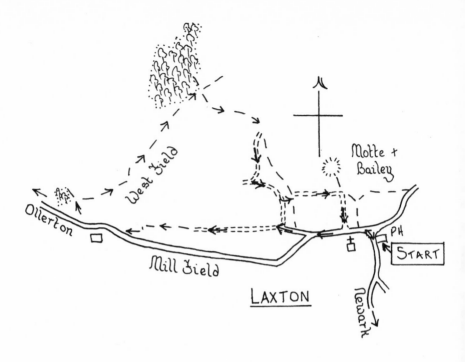

Follow the road onward, passing a large farm. The map calls it Westwood Farm, but the notice outside names a religious house, Beth Shalom. On the bend beyond the farm, turn right, following a clear path (not waymarked) beside the hedge. On reaching a footpath sign, opposite a wood, turn right over a footbridge. Cross straight over the field to a stile, then follow the hedge on the left of the next long field, bearing left with the track and then keeping some way to the right of the hedge. Where the main track veers rightward up the rise, bear left to maintain your position relative to the wooded dip on the left and following a fainter track. Pass through a farm gate and follow the field side, continuing in the same general direction.

Cross a fence (no stile) beside a wood and cross the next field. A gated footbridge will be seen to the left, crossing a stream. Turn your back on this bridge and follow a neglected hedge up the field. Part way up the hill bear left to a stile and footpath sign. Follow the waymarked route over the next very large field. In the extreme right hand corner pass through the gate and follow a farm track around the fields to join a more substantial track leading down to the village. When within sight of the first building on the outskirts of Laxton, leave the track, bearing left to cross a stile and one field. Ignore the stile ahead and, instead, cross the fence on its left to enter a green lane – Back Lane.

Continue until you reach a turning to the right. A diversion over the stile on your left here will bring you onto the site of Laxton Castle. Then back to the stile and follow the lane down to the village.

# ⑪ Old Clipstone
## The Dog and Duck

You will find a genuine welcome at the Dog and Duck, a friendly old village pub in the tiny hamlet of Old Clipstone. The age of the house is uncertain, but it was certainly here 150 years ago when it filled the dual capacity of farm and inn, for the simple reason that neither facility was alone capable of providing a living.

The inn belongs to the Home Brewery (Scottish and Newcastle Breweries), and real ales include both Home Bitter and Theakston XB, with Dry Blackthorn for the cider drinker. Full meals are available lunchtimes and evenings throughout the week, and bar snacks every lunchtime.

There is a traditional three course Sunday lunch, but the popularity of this makes advance booking advisable. Main meals include such delicacies as home-made steak and kidney pie or breaded haddock and beef curry. Bar snacks include Cornish pasty, jumbo sausage, jacket potatoes and various sandwiches. Daily specials are displayed on a blackboard in the bar.

There is a family room, as well as a beer garden and children's play area. The author is witness that parties of walkers are welcome at the Dog and Duck – but it would be sensible to warn the proprietor in advance! Dogs are not welcome inside, for reasons of hygiene, but are not objected to in the garden area.

Telephone: Mansfield (0623) 822138.

*How to get there:* From the A614 Nottingham to Doncaster road, take the B6030, one mile south of the Ollerton roundabout and follow in a south westerly direction for 3 miles. The Dog and Duck is just under the railway bridge on the left hand side of the road.

*Parking:* The inn has a spacious car park, but you are asked to use the bottom spaces if leaving your transport here while you walk, and not to obstruct the proprietor's garage entrance!

*Public transport:* Mansfield to Edwinstowe and Ollerton (Mansfield District).

*Length of the walk:* 5 miles (with optional extension, 6¼ miles). Maps: OS Landranger series 120 Mansfield and the Dukeries, Pathfinder series SK 66/76 Ollerton and SK 46/56 Mansfield North (GR 606649).

*One of the few remaining genuine portions of Sherwood Forest is the Birklands area – the name means birch lands, but you will find many other species here, not least the celebrated English oak. Most visitors join the forest at Edwinstowe, but the walk described here avoids the thickest of the crowds, while still exploring some of the finest parts of the ancient forest. And, if your interest extends to the celebrated Major Oak, an optional extension of just over a mile is well worth the effort.*

**The Walk**

Cross the road from the inn and follow the rough track, Archway Road, directly opposite. The track passes under a bridge and continues ahead into a junction of two railway embankments. Follow the track round left, under the bridge and on over the flood dike to cross the river Maun at Forge Bridge. Continue up the hill, passing the impressive Duke's Archway, a folly built by the Duke of Portland in 1842. Then on through the woods to reach the main Mansfield to Ollerton (A6075) road. Cross and continue on a metalled track, following the forest's edge on the line of the Robin Hood Way. Bear right into the woods with the track, forsaking the Way, which here continues for the time being along the edge of the woods.

Remain with the same track for nearly a mile, ignoring any side tracks, until you reach a broad straight path crossing ahead of you. Turn right here. After following this new track for about ½ mile, an intersecting path is crossed to bring you to a great gnarled oak – the centuries-old Centre Tree.

47

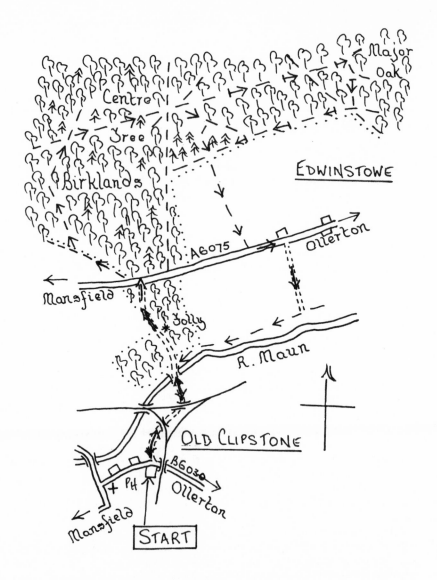

The Centre Tree could perhaps be regarded as the poor relation of the Major Oak, which is one of the forest's honeypots, a mile away from here, at the far end of this same track. But although relatively unknown, this great tree is nevertheless worth a minute or two of your time. An optional extension of rather over a mile will lead you to the Major Oak.

*For the optional extension,* keep straight forward along the same broad track for about a mile, ignoring the two immediate side turnings and, later, a waymarked bridleway crossing left to right. The track, straight throughout, curves to the right towards the end to bring you to the Major Oak.

If you come here – as many visitors do – expecting to see the 'Greenwood Tree' beneath which Robin Hood and his Merry Men foregathered, you are in for a disappointment. For this tree, mighty as it is, certainly was not here in Robin's day. What you will see is the mightiest oak in Sherwood and the 16th largest in the United Kingdom. If you are interested in statistics, its height is 90 ft, its girth 33 ft, and its spread 92 ft. Although the precise age of the Major Oak is not known, it is believed to be between 400 and 500 years old, and might, with care, survive for a further 200 years. This great tree is today being tended with loving care to ensure that it does. Its branches supported by metal ropes and timber posts, and surrounded by a protective fence to keep the visitors at a respectful distance, these efforts are already bearing fruit.

Turn right opposite the Major Oak (passing on the right of a sign 'Visitor Centre 15 minute walk') and follow a secondary, but still distinct path. At a crossways turn right, then immediately bear left, following a bridleway/footpath parallel with the edge of the woods. Keep on along this path until you reach a larch plantation, then look out for the path from the Centre Tree coming in from the right, where you rejoin the main route.

*For the shorter route,* continue on from the Centre Tree for a short distance to reach a three-way junction. Take the track on the right, following the footpath signs. Turn right at the first junction then, soon after, left again at the next, to bring you out to the edge of the forest through a plantation of larches. The path from the Major Oak rejoins the main route here.

Leave the forest, following a fieldside track down to the main road, and turn left. After following the road for a short distance, turn right and follow a lane opposite Villa Real Farm and beside school playing fields. Bear right with the lane, now no more than a track, at the end of the playing fields, resisting the temptation to descend to a bridge over the Maun. Keep straight ahead, and to the right of both the river and the flood dike to follow a delightful woodland path down to the riverside and on to Forge Bridge, from where the route retraces your outward journey, back to the inn.

# ⑫ Bilsthorpe
# The Copper Beech

A modern conversion of a former farmhouse, estimated to be about 160 years old, the inn takes its name from the massive copper beech tree that guards its entrance. Situated in the older part of Bilsthorpe, this busy family pub is popular with both communities – the mining and the farming. The outward aspect of the building is still that of a prosperous yeoman farmer's dwelling; the atmosphere within is smart and modern, and the service prompt and friendly. This is a freehouse, with real ales, including Adnams and Riding, or, if you prefer, Strongbow Cider on draught. Meals and bar snacks are available every day except Sunday, with a full menu to choose from. A speciality here is baked potatoes with a variety of tasty fillings. I came here on a foggy and frosty day at Christmastide, while walking off the effects of overindulgence in turkey – and enjoyed a mouthwatering and huge bacon sarny.

The Copper Beech has a beer garden and a children's play area, as well as a family room, and customers may eat their own food in the garden on non-catering days. Well behaved dogs are welcome, except in the lounge.

Telephone: Mansfield (0623) 870725.

50

*How to get there:* From the A614 Nottingham/Ollerton road, turn east 1½ miles north of the A617 roundabout and follow this road through the mining village, turning right at the end to reach Old Bilsthorpe. The Copper Beech is on the right, just beyond the parish church.

*Parking:* A spacious car park is provided here, where you may leave your transport for the duration of your walk.

*Public transport:* Buses run between Newark, Bilsthorpe and Mansfield (East Midland), also Bilsthorpe and Newark (Lincolnshire Road Car).

*Length of the walk:* 4¾ miles. Maps: OS Landranger series 120 Mansfield and the Dukeries, Pathfinder series SK 66/76 Ollerton and SK 65/75 Newark on Trent West (GR 652601).

*Despite Bilsthorpe's long industrial tradition – both coal and oil have been produced in the locality for many years – this is essentially a purely rural walk. We first cross, by field paths and ancient trackways, to the neighbouring village of Eakring, where we visit a memorial to a man who many – including the writer – regard as a saint, but who was treated as a leper when he came to this area. We return to Bilsthorpe by well-defined byways offering extensive views over central Nottinghamshire, and passing close by Brail Wood.*

**The Walk**
Follow the village road north past Church Hill, turning right at a filling station. Beyond the few houses the road declines to the status of a rough lane. Where it bends rightward, cross a stile on the left and follow the track beyond, crossing a metalled road (Brailwood Road) and continuing along the enclosed track opposite, with the landfill site on your right, until you reach a wood (Brail Wood).

Turn left and follow the waymarked footpath beside the wood. On reaching the end of the trees bear right over the ensuing field, making for the leftward end of a distant row of birch trees. At the far side of the field, cross the gap into the next field and again bear right, now heading for an angle in the hedge opposite. Then follow the hedge to the right before passing through to join and follow an overgrown hollow way. This secret little path climbs out into the far corner of the field, leading you onto a farm track.

Cross an intersecting lane and continue forward, now along an enclosed lane, in the direction of Eakring. After a short distance, leave the track by a little path on the left, signposted for 'Mompesson Cross'.

At the top of a little rise you will come to a small stone cross in a fenced enclosure. This is Mompesson Cross. The inscription tells us, baldly, that 'Near this spot stood Pulpit Ash, where Mompesson

51

preached on coming to Eakring as Rector in 1670, after leaving Eyam in Derbyshire which had been decimated by the plague'. The story of Eyam is well known, as is the part played by William Mompesson in confining the infection to his own village. Less familiar is the treatment meted out to this good man years later, when he came to Eakring, where the superstitious villagers denied him access to the village – or its church. Hence the Pulpit Ash. There is a simple seat here, beside

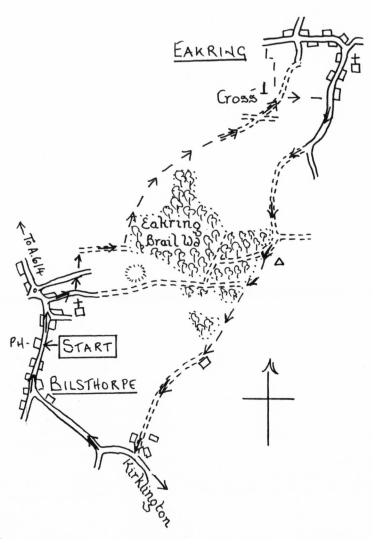

the cross, where you may sit for a space and enjoy the views over Eakring village and the surrounding countryside.

Return to the main track. By turning left you can reach the village, where the Saville Arms will provide liquid refreshment. Otherwise, cross the lane and follow the waymarked path (Robin Hood Way) beside the field and round to the right to enter an enclosed path leading down to Side Lane and the Kirklington road. Turn right.

On the bend at the end of the village, take the lane (Brail Lane) on the right. Where the track branches, take the leftward way and continue uphill, ignoring a bridlepath on the left close to the summit. When level with the trig point, pause and look around you. You are only 370 ft above sea-level here, but the views are superb.

At the entrance to Brail Wood, cast off left to follow the bridlepath on the left of the wood, continuing on around the angle of the wood. The route marked on the OS map crosses the field from here diagonally, cutting the corner, but you may find that common usage follows the edge of the wood right round. Carry on from here to the left of Fox Holes Wood and round the edge of the field to join a hard track and pass to the right of a farmhouse. Follow the lane from here to reach a collection of semi-industrial buildings at Belle Eau Park. Turn right and follow the road round, past Wycar Leys, to Bilsthorpe.

# ⑬ Kirkby in Ashfield
## The Duke of Wellington

Although Kirkby is an industrial town with a long tradition of coal mining, its western edge – the old village – still retains the air of a typical Derbyshire border village. The 'Duke' stands in the old village, hard by the parish church, and has the outward appearance of a traditional village inn. The interior is tastefully modern – the author's attention was particularly taken by a print of a sailing ship, matched elsewhere in the lounge by a model sailing ship. Both items rather out of place perhaps in a house dedicated to a famous military leader, but the army – and its uniforms – are also featured pictorially. We found no horse brasses here – but we did spot various items of bric-a-brac peeping cheekily from the top of certain of the beams! The inn was once the home of a butcher, who plied his trade in a neighbouring building while his wife sold ales from the house. I am told that the inn has a resident ghost – a latter-day one, apparently, called Fred, who smokes heavily and throws things around!

This is one of Mansfield Brewery's houses, and real ales include Riding and Old Baily. Food is available every lunchtime and evening, with a wide range of hot meals and bar snacks. House specials include The Duke's Special, a steak sandwich served on a crouton slice, and

The Duke's Mixed Grill – 4oz rump steak, 4oz gammon, lamb chop, liver and 2 Lincolnshire sausages.
The house has a non-smoking area, beer garden and children's play area. Well behaved dogs are welcome, in the taproom only.
Telephone: Mansfield (0623) 753044.

*How to get there:* From the A60 (Nottingham to Mansfield) or the A611 (Hucknall to Mansfield) roads, follow the B6020 west through Kirkby town centre. At a T junction turn left, onto the B6018, and the Duke is a little way along on the left, before the parish church.

*Parking:* The inn has a large car park at the rear.

*Public transport:* Buses (Trent) run from all the main local towns – Nottingham, Mansfield, Ripley, Alfreton and Chesterfield.

*Length of the walk:* 4 miles. Maps: OS Landranger series 120 Mansfield and the Dukeries, Pathfinder series SK 45/55 Sutton in Ashfield (GR 490560).

*This walk takes us quickly out of the town, descending through pleasant rural terrain to reach the delightful recreational woodland of Portland Park. Then by field paths and past the forbidding precincts of Bentinck Colliery to return, via quiet country ways, and over the infant river Erewash, to Kirkby.*

## The Walk

Pass by the church, taking extreme care – there is no footpath so keep close in to the wall – and leave the road immediately by the waymarked footpath on the left. A good clear path leads over the fields, passing to the left of a graveyard. At the end of the field continue round to the left and cross the old railway track, passing to the left of a white cottage and bearing right away from the track to follow a waymarked path along the left hand edge of the field. Ascend an embankment by steps and cross another disused railway line, descending again to cross two fields and the infant river Erewash. Cross a working railway (carefully!) and enter woodland.

You are in the Portland Park Visitor Centre, a very popular local beauty spot. There are various waymarked woodland paths here and a children's play area, as well as toilets and sometimes refreshment facilities. A good spot to bring the family, and you will be forgiven if you simply walk over from Kirkby, spend an hour or two here, and walk back – but do take care when crossing that railway!

Pass the toilets, leaving the park by a waymarked footpath on the right and climbing up to the fields. Cross diagonally to a stile, over a

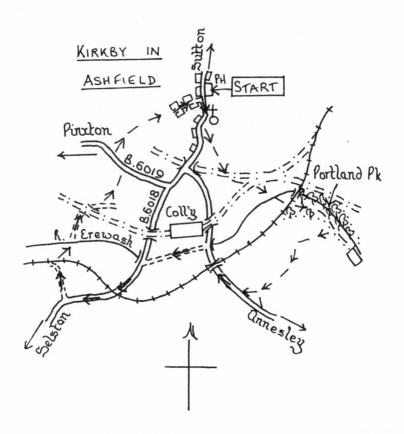

lane and, through the farm gate, turn right to follow the hedge. At the end of this field turn left along the nearside of the hedge. Follow the field boundary over two fields, then descend steeply and cross the field diagonally to the right to reach the road, and turn right. Follow the road under a narrow bridge and turn left, just before Bentinck Colliery, onto a rough track, not the most attractive part of the walk, but short – and unavoidable.

At the next road turn left, climbing the hill over the level crossing. On the bend beyond a pair of houses, turn right. Follow the way-marked path as far as the railway, where the track bends. If there is an ash heap here, clamber round it and pass through the handgate, crossing the line and emerging, via a second handgate, onto a farm track. Turn right and follow the track, keeping your eyes well peeled for your exit path. It is not far along, but neither is it particularly obvious. Look for a pair of tall concrete posts on the left. The path passes between them and leads onto fields. Follow the hedge round to the right to cross the river Erewash and a couple of stiles, then cross the next field diagonally right to a stile in the corner, by the field gate.

Go along the farm lane past the farm and round to the right, passing under the railway bridge. At a gateway onto the open fields turn left, crossing the field diagonally and heading just to the right of an electricity pylon. Cross a stile and continue, under the power line, following the field boundary over two fields to reach the road.

Turn left along the road, for a short distance only, leaving again by a stile beside a half-concealed guide post on the right. Cross the field direct, making for a bush at the top end – you will find a first-class stile lurking behind it. Ascend over the next field, bearing slightly right. The lie of the land prevents you seeing the exit stile until you are over the rise. Cross the stile and continue beside the hedge over one short field, then bear right, still following hedges left and right along a developing lane and gravitating onto a line for Kirkby parish church. Emerge onto a metalled lane and follow through to Manor House Court, and Church Street.

# ⑭ Blidworth
# The Bird in Hand

The village of Blidworth is inextricably linked with the Robin Hood legends. Maid Marion is reputed to have been born, and Will Scarlet buried, here. And Fountain Dale, nearby, was the site of Robin's first encounter with the redoubtable Friar Tuck. The village's other claim to fame is the annual 'Rocking Ceremony', which takes place each year in the parish Church of the Presentation, and in which the village's most recently born baby stars.

The Bird in Hand is set back from the road, and its more attractive aspect is from the rear of the premises. But its undoubtedly plain exterior, when seen from the road, belies the cheerful and welcoming interior. This inn is unusual, too, in that the comfortable lounge extends around three sides of the bar. The Bird in Hand stands on the hilltop, commanding magnificent views over the surrounding countryside, views which can be enjoyed equally from the comfort of the lounge or, in fair weather, from the well equipped garden/play area.

This is one of Mansfield Brewery's houses, and the ales on offer include Old Baily and Riding Traditional Bitter. Strongbow Cider is available on draught. The inn offers a wide selection of bar meals,

salads and sandwiches, not to mention a daily choice of home-made pies, baked on the premises. Evening meals are available too and, if you come between 5.30 and 7.00 pm, you can have two meals for the price of one. Food is not provided on Sundays, but there is no objection to patrons eating their own food, in the garden area only, on those days. Well behaved dogs are welcome.
Telephone: Mansfield (0623) 792356.

*How to get there:* Blidworth is a large hilltop village on the B6020 road between Kirkby in Ashfield and Farnsfield. If approaching via the A60 Nottingham to Mansfield road, turn east at the Larch Farm crossroads. Blidworth is about 2½ miles along this road, and the inn will be found on the right as you enter the village.

*Parking:* Parking is not easy in Blidworth itself, but the inn has a roomy car park of its own, in which you are welcome to park for the duration of your stay in the area.

*Public transport:* Blidworth is served by Trent buses between Nottingham, Hucknall and Mansfield, and from Sutton in Ashfield.

*Length of the walk:* 4¼ miles. Maps: OS Landranger series 120 Mansfield and the Dukeries, Pathfinder series SK 45/55 Sutton in Ashfield (GR 587556).

*This walk takes us first through fields of 'unimproved' grassland and along sandy lanes to Fountain Dale, where we stroll through ancient woodland which would have been familiar, many centuries ago, to Friar Tuck. Then by peaceful byways (good blackberrying ground in late summer) we go back to Blidworth village.*

**The Walk**
Leave Blidworth by the Kirkby Road, taking the first turning, Ricket Lane, on your right. A stile on the left here will take you across the front of a private dwelling and into a narrow enclosed way, leading out to the open fields.

An intimate field path follows, crossing a series of small unimproved fields, all following the same general direction but crossing with regular frequency from one side to the other of the intervening hedgerow. These are 'old-fashioned' fields, untouched by modern technology and host to ragwort, mushrooms (or toadstools?), and the calling cards of horses. After a mile or so the path negotiates larger fields, some of which may be carrying arable crops. Look out for the yellow arrows, and follow these faithfully around the perimeter of these fields to pass alongside a wood and reach a narrow enclosed lane.

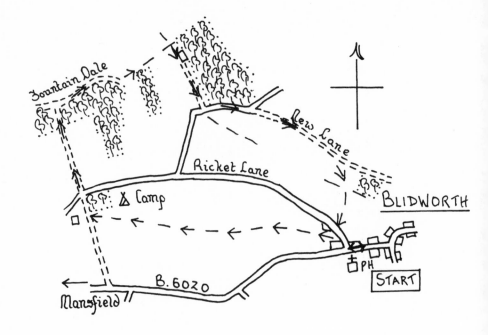

Turn right along the track, crossing Ricket Lane, close to the Robin Hood Scout Camp, and continue on over the fields as the track descends into a belt of woodland, to reach Fountain Dale. This was traditionally the scene of Robin Hood's first embarrassing encounter with Friar Tuck, when the outlaw was tumbled into the stream (Rainworth Water) by the sturdy friar. The stream and its ponds are dried up now and the dale is overgrown. But there is supposedly a moat still here in the woods, and Friar Tuck's Well is marked on the map, but you will have your work cut out to locate either of these sites.

On reaching a broad track turn right, following the path through the wooded dale, and bearing slightly right at a junction of paths to follow the hedgeside. After leaving the woods, continue over a large field with considerable beds of rosebay willow herb. On reaching a cross-path turn right, and pass through the woods, crossing the streambed to reach Providence Farm.

Keep to the path on the right of the buildings to emerge onto the farm lane. Follow this to the road and turn left. Continue along the road for some distance until, at a leftward bend, an unmetalled track will be met leading straight ahead. Follow this new lane for a good ½ mile, then go over a stile on your right and cross two fields diagonally to reach a stile and gate in the dip. Cross the stile and walk past the gate – do not go through. Continue up the hill, following the hedge, to rejoin Ricket Lane, close to your starting point.

# ⑮ Upton
## The Cross Keys

The charming old village of Upton counts among its treasures one of the most splendid church towers in the county. Crowned with eight pinnacles clustered around a ninth (The Nine Disciples), the structure incorporates a priests's room with a fireplace, and holes in the walls where doves once nested. Also worthy of mention is the local headquarters of the British Horological Institute which are, on occasion, open to visitors.

The Cross Keys, a listed building, was formerly a farmhouse, built about 300 years ago. More correctly, it is a collection of buildings, now amalgamated into one, extending back from the road and betraying their agricultural origins. Alterations have been carried out sympathetically and in such a way as to emphasise, rather than belittle, the traditional atmosphere. To this end, a log burning open fire has been reintroduced in winter and quarry tiles revealed, a new taproom added, incorporating carved pews from Newark parish church, and a former dovecote has been converted into a restaurant.

This is a freehouse, and the real ales include Boddingtons, Brakspear, Marston's Pedigree, Bateman XXXB and regular guest beers. Food is available through the week, lunchtimes and evenings, snacks as well as full meals. The scope of the menu is impressive, and some idea of the range available will be gathered from the fact that the choice of sandwiches alone is the most imaginative we have come across in our travels, and includes Colston Bassett stilton, roast sirloin, chicken liver paté, egg and cress, and tuna and sweetcorn.

Children are welcome in the taproom, the restaurant and the garden area, which also serves as the beer garden. You are not expected to picnic in the garden or elsewhere – but with such a selection of delicacies on offer it would be surprising if you even considered it! Dogs – well behaved ones – are welcome.

Telephone: Southwell (0636) 813269.

*How to get there:* Easy! Upton is a linear village, on the A612 road between Southwell and Newark, and the Cross Keys is on the Main Street at the western end of the village.

*Parking:* Ample parking is available in the pub car park, which you are welcome to use while walking.

*Public transport:* Mansfield District buses (Mansfield – Southwell – Newark), Pathfinder (Newark – Southwell), and Trent (Nottingham – Southwell – Newark).

*Length of the walk:* 4¾ miles. Maps: OS Landranger series 120 Mansfield and the Dukeries, Pathfinder series SK 65/75 Newark on Trent West (GR 735543).

*The footpaths and byways of Upton and district are well marked but, if our observations are accurate, lightly trod. This we find surprising, because the quality of the walking, which includes a sizeable section of the Trent Valley Way, is excellent. But do not take our word for it – come along with us and enjoy the hills, woods and ways for yourself. Just one word of warning: do not put too much faith in the Pathfinder map here. Many of the paths have been diverted, and one complete section of wood has disappeared without trace! But don't worry, you'll be safe following my directions!*

**The Walk**
Follow the road east, right through the village and beyond. As it bends rightward, pass through a farm gateway on the left and follow the Trent Valley Way path, first crossing the field diagonally to reach a stream crossing, then continuing straight ahead over the succeeding two fields, heading directly for the top of Micklebarrow Hill. At the summit bear right though a line of hedgerow trees to reach and cross a stile in the extreme corner of the field.

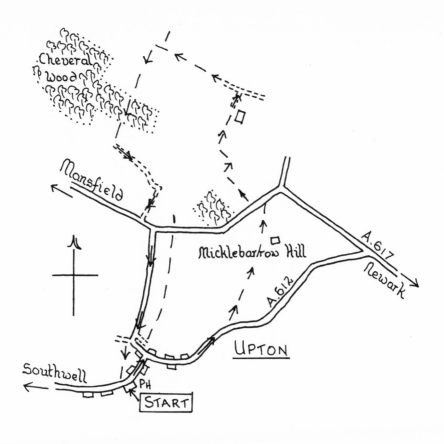

Walk with the fence on your left, crossing another stile and
continuing, now on the left of the fence. Follow the meanderings of
the fence past a private tennis court, bearing left over the field to reach
a gateway, then on across the corner of a second field to cross a stile
and reach the road. Go over the road and turn left.

Leave the road again by a stile and footbridge on the right and
continue on the left of the hedge. Turn right with the hedge at its end,
then left along the facing hedge to reach and pass through a gap. Turn
left along the hedge, then right in the next field, and follow the hedge-
side to a farm, turning left there onto a track. Follow left, then right,
past a wood (screening the farm buildings) and meet a T junction.

Turn left onto a green lane, leaving the Trent Valley Way. At the end
of the lane, cross a stile and continue on the succeeding field path for
the length of one very long field. Turn left through the gate at the end

and follow a farm track all the way to Cheveral Wood.

Follow the footpath into the wood, passing through a gate on your right at the far side and continuing ahead, with the hedge on your left. Go through another gate at the end, turning left into a pleasant green lane. Follow the lane south east, then south west, to reach the road at Spring Wood Farm. Turn left.

At the Upton road turn right, following the road to the outskirts of the village. On the bend by the first houses, keep straight ahead and join a footpath, passing to the right of derelict buildings and the wall of Upton Hall, then along an enclosed path to reach the road. Turn left here, back to the inn.

# ⑯ Southwell
## The Bramley Apple

There is a popular misconception that the possession of a cathedral confers the status of 'city' on a town; if this were correct, Southwell would probably be the smallest city in England. As it is, it is certainly the only village – albeit a big one – to boast a cathedral, the magnificent 11th century Southwell Minster. Southwell's other claim to fame is the Bramley Apple, which originated here and from which our host inn takes its name.

The Bramley Apple, in Church Street, is a quiet, unpretentious pub, away from the mainstream of Southwell life yet only a short distance from the town centre. The inn is two centuries old, and the decor – as might be expected in a house dedicated to the Bramley – largely features the apple. The service is pleasant and courteous.

The Bramley is a freehouse and the ales include Bateman, Pedigree and guest beers. Both Woodpecker and Old English Cider are available on draught. Food is available daily at lunchtimes and every evening except Sunday and Monday. The menu is often changed and can include such dishes as deep fried plaice, spare ribs, beef in garlic and horseradish sauce, chicken Kiev, braised leg of pork, pork chop and roast pork – and the size of the servings is almost daunting.

The bar is basically just one large room, with the rearward section partitioned off for smoke-free eating. Well behaved dogs are welcome in the bar area. Accommodation is available here. Telephone: Southwell (0636) 813675.

*How to get there:* The bustling township of Southwell is situated on the A612 road about 13 miles from Nottingham and 7 from Newark. Church Street branches off the main shopping street directly opposite the ancient half-timbered Saracen's Head Inn, and the Bramley Apple is a good ¼ mile along here, past the Minster and the car park.

*Parking:* Parking at the inn is absolutely minimal, although there are no restrictions on kerb-side parking in the immediate vicinity. There is, however, a large free public car park only ¼ mile away – also on Church Street and opposite the Minster entrance – which you are recommended to use.

*Public transport:* Southwell is well served with buses between Nottingham and Newark (Pathfinder) and from Mansfield to Newark (Mansfield District).

*Length of the walk:* 4 miles. Maps: OS Landranger series 120 Mansfield and the Dukeries, Pathfinder series SK 65/75 Newark on Trent West (GR 705538).

*We leave Southwell town centre by quiet footways, and visit the orchards of one of the district's biggest fruit growers. Come in September for the magnificent sight of the trees in fruit (you will find it hard to resist the temptation to help yourself!). We continue along the Southwell Trail, a former railway track now converted to a footpath and bridleway; then on beside the humble river Greet before returning, by field and footway, to our starting point.*

**The Walk**
Leaving the Bramley Apple, follow Church Street past the Minster, turning right at the Saracen's Head and then left again onto Queen Street. Opposite the Rope Walk turn left, as though entering the Saracen's Head car park, and bear right to join and follow an enclosed footpath beside a school. Stick with the metalled path around two sides of the school field. At the end of the field, cross an intersecting path and continue straight on through a wooded area, bearing left to follow the fence and a succeeding path between hedges.
Cross a stile and continue through the fields, keeping to the left all the way. After crossing a road the path continues, still to the right of

67

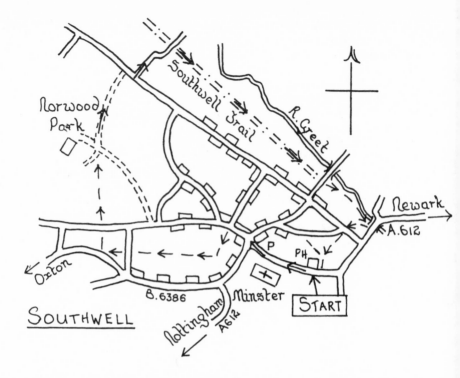

the hedge and a metalled track, heading for an old cottage.

Just short of the cottage, resist the temptation to join the adjacent road, and turn sharp right, heading for a stile (but no accompanying fence) and a slab over the roadside ditch. Cross the road and follow the waymarked footpath through Norwood Park, a fine green track between orchards and nursery crops. On reaching a junction with a metalled estate road – privately owned Norwood Hall can be seen away to your left – cross the hall drive and bear right a little, passing a couple of 'Packhouse' signs, and follow the lane down to a road.

Turn right along the road and, after passing a house, turn left along a side road, signposted for 'Maythorne'. Soon after negotiating a double bend, turn right onto the trackbed of the former Southwell/ Farnsfield Railway line (Southwell Trail).

Follow the pleasant trail through to Station Road. On reaching the road, cross over, bearing left to enter the Riverside Estate. Just short of the first houses, descend a run of steps to join the riverside walk, a metalled footway beside the river Greet, and follow this through to the A612 (Newark) road. Turn right, passing The Gatehouse.

Go through a handgate between the house and a stream and follow the ensuing little footpath. Cross a stile, and turn left over a footbridge to enter the Greet Park Estate. Follow the estate road system through to Newark Road. Cross the road, bearing right to reach the corner of Burgage Lane. The streamside path is rejoined in the angle of the road junction. Follow the path over the fields, keeping close to the stream until after a bridge is passed, then bear slightly right as the path branches, to reach an enclosed footway crossing right to left. Turn left, crossing the stream and continue down the footway (Shady Lane) to reach Church Street. Turn right to the Bramley Apple.

# ⑰ Moorgreen
# The Horse and Groom

The Horse and Groom occupies a prominent position on the B600 road between Nuthall and Underwood. This attractive building was one of many recommended to us for the quality of food and drink, allied with good service, and our experience fully confirmed that recommendation. The Horse and Groom is a busy and spacious inn, the interior decor reflecting the equestrian theme of the house's title. Brasses, saddlery, harness and racing colours decorate the popular lounge with, to add a certain contrary touch, a frame of pugilistic cigarette cards.

This is a Kimberley Inn, and open daily from 11 am through to 11 pm. Among a wide selection of liquid refreshments you may, according to your taste, drink Classic Bitter or Strongbow Draught Cider. Food, too, is available seven days a week, from 11 am to 9 pm, with bar snacks or full meals (including a children's and a vegetarian menu) in the downstairs bars, as well as a separate restaurant upstairs. Meals include gammon steaks, breaded plaice, lasagne and scampi, while those of simpler taste can settle for chip or sausage burgers, or meat roll and chips.

The Horse and Groom is a house to suit all tastes, having a family

room, beer garden, children's area and a no-smoking zone. Well behaved dogs are welcome too.
Telephone: Alfreton (0773) 713417.

*How to get there:* From the A610 Nottingham to Ripley road, take the B600 turning at the Nuthall roundabout, ½ mile east of the M1 junction (26), passing under the motorway and turning right by Nuthall church. Continue through Watnall until you reach the B6010 junction, left. The inn is directly opposite, on the corner of New Road.

*Parking:* The inn has a spacious car park (entrance on New Road) which you are welcome to use while you take your walk.

*Public transport:* Buses (Trent) run from Nottingham, Alfreton and Hucknall.

*Length of the walk:* 4½ miles. Maps: OS Landranger series 129 Nottingham and Loughborough, Pathfinder series SK 44/54 Nottingham North and Ilkeston (GR 485476).

*Beauvale is a district of saints and sinners. This is D.H. Lawrence country and it requires no great feats of imagination to visualise Lady Chatterley and her game-keeper lover at play in the woods hereabouts. But these are fictional sinners. Long before Lawrence's day, Beauvale was the home of more pious men. Here, in pre-reformation days, stood the Carthusian Priory of Beauvale, and it was from here that Priors Houghton and Laurence set out on their last sad journey, to martyrdom at Tyburn. Little survives of the priory today, although pilgrimages still take place from time to time. But although scheduled as an ancient monument, there is today no general right of access and we must be content to view the site from afar and settle for a delightful woodland walk − keeping a weather eye open for Mr Mellors and his lady, of course!*

**The Walk**
Follow the B600 road north west from the inn to reach the entrance gate to Beauvale House. A bridleway enters the side gate and follows the drive, leaving after a while to follow a simpler track, flanked by rhododendrons, through the woods beside Moorgreen Reservoir.

Follow the reservoir-side track for the best part of a mile, the lake petering out to a stream. The most direct route here remains with the main track, but a pleasanter diversion follows a pretty streamside bridleway on the left. On rejoining the original track, double back right, up the hill, to reach and cross a stile into the fields.

Follow the waymarked 'Misk Hills' path alongside the hedge to your left. The Pathfinder map depicts the path as following the right of the

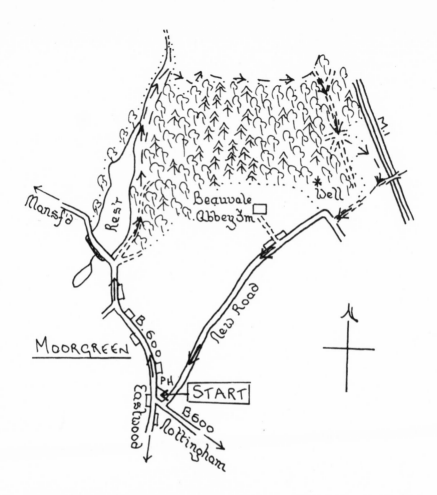

hedge, but optical evidence confirms it is on the left side! At the end of the field turn left, following the path around two sides of the wood and merging with a broad track from Underwood. Enjoy the splendid views over open country here towards Annesley.

Turn right into the woods on reaching a footpath sign. The OS map depicts the right of way as following a line a little to the west of the broad track, but popular usage (and the lack of any clearly defined or waymarked route) favours the main track. At the top of the rise a second path merges in from the left, to continue ahead, now gently descending a firmer trackway. Soon after bending rightwards with the track, turn left at a junction of paths and immediately reach a second, three-way junction. Take the leftmost of the tracks – waymarked with yellow plastic arrows here and there – and follow through to a stile, and the end of the woods.

Take the footpath alongside the hedge on the left of the field, continuing beside the motorway. Ignore a side turning here, leading to a footbridge over the motorway, and continue by the fieldside to reach a broad track alongside the wood. Follow this track down to a stile, and the road.

In the woods, close to here, is Robin Hood's Well. In fact, it had nothing to do with the outlaw, and probably belonged to the priory. It can be located, by a diligent search. However, although the public appear to roam pretty freely through these woods, I am told that away from the paths already described, they are private.

Follow the road down from here all the way back to the inn, passing by the entrance to Beauvale Abbey Farm. As you leave the woods behind, the farm, with the remaining walls of the ancient priory, will be seen over the fields to the right of the road.

# ⑱ Thurgarton
## The Coach and Horses

The first impression gained as you enter the public bar of the grey-stone Coach and Horses will be the cheerful ambience of the place, the friendly bar staff and the sociable company. Owned by the Scottish and Newcastle Breweries, the house was founded in 1801, a fact proudly proclaimed upon a mirror in the roomy bar. The oak beams, half-timbering effect, refectory tables and wall-bench seating all contribute to the cosy and welcoming atmosphere.

You will be able to drink Theakston XB and Home Bitter here, or, if you prefer, Old English Draught Cider. Food is provided daily – lunchtimes only – except on Mondays. The rolls, with ham, beef or cheese, and with or without salad, are each a meal in themselves – of gigantic proportions and very filling. The inn has a beer garden and children's area and well behaved dogs are welcome.

Telephone: Southwell (0636) 830257.

*How to get there:* The attractive village of Thurgarton is on the main

A612 Nottingham to Newark road, between Lowdham and Southwell. The Coach and Horses is on the eastern side of the road, in the centre of the village.

*Parking:* The inn has its own roomy car park, and patrons are welcome to leave their vehicles here for the duration of their walk.

*Public transport:* Trent bus service between Nottingham, Southwell and Newark calls here. British Rail's Nottingham, Newark and Lincoln service stops at Thurgarton station, ½ mile outside the village.

*Length of the walk:* 4 miles. Maps: OS Landranger series 129 Nottingham and Loughborough and 120 Mansfield and the Dukeries, Pathfinder series SK 64/74 Carlton and Elston and SK 65/75 Newark on Trent West (GR 695492).

*This gem of a walk takes us over an easy circular route, along quiet lanes and bridleways around the former priory lands to the west of Thurgarton village. Formerly livestock grazing – as confirmed by the presence along the way of an ancient sheep dip – the fields are now wholly arable. The paths are clear and easy to follow and there are no stiles to climb.*

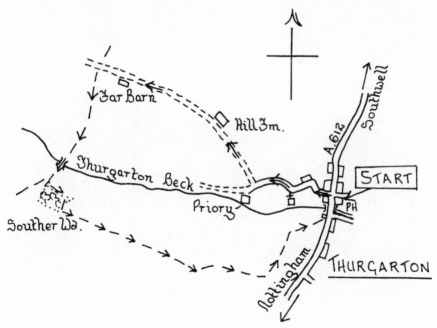

## The Walk

Take the road opposite the inn (The Hollows), ascending an elevated path on the left of the road with a high wall on its left. The path descends again to rejoin the road, bearing right on a bend by the church and continuing steadily uphill. At the entrance to Checkers Farm turn right, following a concrete lane.

Thurgarton was formerly the home of a priory. The original building no longer exists and its replacement – a secular one – belongs to a world famous pharmaceutical firm. The company is clearly anxious to ensure that nobody is left in any doubt as to the privacy of the premises and you will notice a proliferation of prohibitive signs.

Follow the lane, passing Hill Farm and continuing straight ahead. The lane reverts to an unsurfaced state, with low hedges and broad views over the surrounding countryside. Pass a group of barns to the left of the track and, at the end of the next field (there is no intersecting hedge), turn left at a bridleway arrow, following a broad field track over one large field before bearing right to cross Thurgarton Beck by an interesting little stone-parapeted bridge, with a former sheep-dipping area beside it. Continue ahead, ignoring a turning to the right, and following the left hand side of the hedge to reach Souther Wood.

Turn left, following the edge of the wood as far as a handgate on the right. Passing through the gate, cross a short arm of the wood and continue on, still with the wood on your right and a field on your left. Turn left at the end of this field.

Follow an excellent bridleway from here, beside the hedge, over five fields with interconnecting handgates. At the end of the fifth field bear left, still following the hedge, over this and the succeeding very large field, then swinging left to follow a residual field boundary past a group of three trees, with the church tower straight ahead.

Just short of the priory grounds, pass through a handgate on the right, and follow a field path at right angles to the one you have left. Bear left with the path to reach a handgate leading into an enclosed path and follow this down to the road, by the priory entrance.

# ⑲ Epperstone
## The Cross Keys

Mine Host at the Cross Keys is justly proud of his inn's status as the only Nottinghamshire inn to have been featured in all 20 editions of the CAMRA National Good Beer Guide – which identified the house as a reminder of what a good village pub should be. And the combination here of good ales, fine food and first class facilities fully justifies that recommendation.

A solid, four-square building – one of Hardys and Hansons' houses – you will find no fancy modern falderals here, just a typical, honest-to-goodness traditional village pub, with old beams, wall-plates, brasses, and photographs of old village and rural scenes – and a sociable landlord with friendly and courteous staff.

Real ales are all cask conditioned, both bitter and mild, and include Kimberley Classic and Strong Premium Bitter. Strongbow Cider is available on draught. Food is provided, lunchtime and evening, from Tuesday to Saturday, and Sunday lunchtime. The speciality of the house, on an impressive menu, is the home-made pies. And I would recommend the superb steak and kidney pie as an experience not to be missed! The Cross Keys has both a beer garden and a family room,

as well as a garden area for the children, and well behaved dogs are welcome in the bar.
Telephone: Nottingham (0602) 663033.

*How to get there:* The Cross Keys is situated in the centre of the charming old village of Epperstone, just off the A6097 Bingham/Oxton link road, between Lowdham and Oxton.

*Parking:* The inn has a vast parking area where you may leave your car for an hour or two – but ask first.

*Public transport:* Epperstone is served by buses between Nottingham and Oxton, operated jointly by Trent, Barton and Pathfinder.

*Length of the walk:* 5¾ miles. Maps: OS Landranger series 129 Nottingham and Loughborough and 120 Mansfield and the Dukeries, Pathfinder series SK 64/74 Carlton and Elston and SK 65/75 Newark on Trent West (GR 653485).

*The pretty village of Epperstone is justly popular with visitors, and a centre for many pleasant rural walks over the gently rolling hills of central Nottinghamshire. This walk is entirely rural, steering clear, from start to finish, of anything greater than a farmhouse, and keeping to country pathways, bridlepaths and farm roads, and by fields, dumbles (the local name for a small wooded dale) and the occasional small wood.*

**The Walk**
Follow the road east from the inn, turning left onto Hagg Lane and continuing around the double bend and on up the ensuing hill. On the hilltop, cross a plank bridge and stile on the left (taking care not to fall into the ditch) and follow the waymarked path on the left of the hedge. Go round the end of the field to cross a footbridge and continue round again to the right, still keeping to the field's edge. Partway over this second field, turn right over a stile and double back along the opposite side of the hedge. Turn left around the corner of the field and follow the hedge for the full length of this very long field, climbing over the hill. It is worth your while to pause on reaching the highest point to look back. There is a superb view from here back over Epperstone and the Trent Valley.

Follow the hedge around the end of the field and through into the next field, again following the left of the hedge in the same direction as before. At the end of the field, cross the dumble and turn right, following the diverted route of the path around the field and over the rise to reach a derelict building on the site of Lady Well. Follow the

79

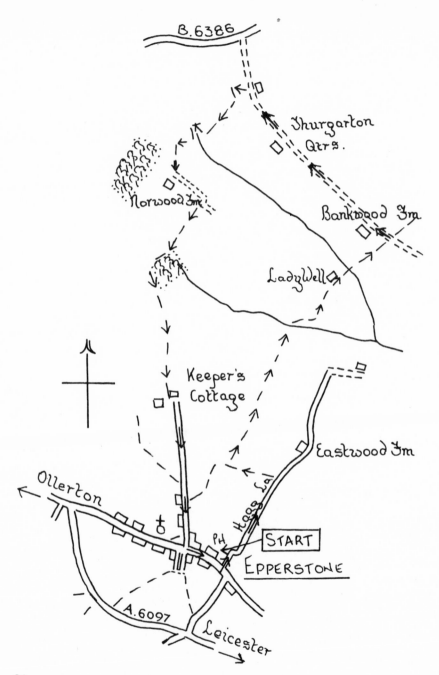

B.6386

Thurgarton
Qtrs.

Bankwood Fm

Norwood Fm

LadyWell

Keeper's
Cottage

Eastwood Fm

Ollerton

PH

START
EPPERSTONE

A.6097

Leicester

cart track through a belt of woodland and reach an enclosed track (accessed via a rusty metal gate). Ascend to the wooded hilltop and arrive at an enclosed farm lane.

Turn left along the lane, bearing right through Bankwood Farm and continuing on along the metalled lane, past Thurgarton Quarters Farm.

By Argyll Cottage and close to Halloughton Dumble, turn left onto a waymarked bridlepath through woodland, distinguished by a pair of unusually decorative wooden gateposts. Emerging onto fields, turn sharp left, following the perimeter of the field all the way round to the dumble and on, passing through to the opposite side of the dumble on reaching the end of the woods and continuing left, still following the perimeter of the field.

Beyond the end of the woods, join a gravel track and keep on ahead, bearing left as you approach Norwood Farm. On the second bend from here, leave the gravel track and continue straight ahead on a green track beside the hedge. Cross the dumble and pass to the right of a wood, turning left at the end, still keeping the wood on your left and, later, a hedge on your right, with widening views ahead over the Trent Valley.

Follow this superb track by field and wood to Keeper's Cottage, and bear left to join the road. Follow this down to Epperstone, then turn left in the village for the inn.

# 20 Caythorpe
## The Black Horse

An attractive white-painted traditional village inn in the centre of the quiet little old-world village of Caythorpe, the Black Horse dates from the early 18th century – and counts among its former patrons the notorious Dick Turpin. The decor features oak beams and half timbering, with a variety of brasses, chinaware and wild-life pictures in the cosy lounge.

This is a Greenalls/Shipstone's house, with both Shipstone's and Tetley real ales, as well as Scrumpy Jack Cider. Food is provided daily and in the evenings from Monday to Saturday and you can choose from a full menu which includes a wide variety of grills, salads, fish dishes and snacks; or you may, if you wish, opt for a late breakfast. Daily specials include curry, liver (an unusual but welcome option), and fresh cod or plaice. There is an outside children's area and beer garden, and well behaved dogs are welcome.

Telephone: Nottingham (0602) 663520.

*How to get there:* Caythorpe lies close to the northern bank of the river Trent and to the south of the A612 Nottingham to Southwell road. The village is best approached from either the A612 or the A6097

(Bingham/Oxton link), via Lowdham station. Turn east immediately to the south of the station crossing. Caythorpe is about a mile from here, and the Black Horse is on the left, in the village.

*Parking:* The inn has its own car park which you are welcome to use while taking your walk. Alternatively, there is a parking area alongside the riverside road between Caythorpe and Hoveringham.

*Public transport:* Caythorpe is served by Trent buses, Nottingham – Southwell – Newark, and British Rail (Lowdham, 1 mile), Nottingham – Newark – Lincoln.

*Length of the walk:* 4¼ miles. Maps: OS Landranger series 129 Nottingham and Loughborough, Pathfinder series SK 64/74 Carlton and Elston (GR 689455).

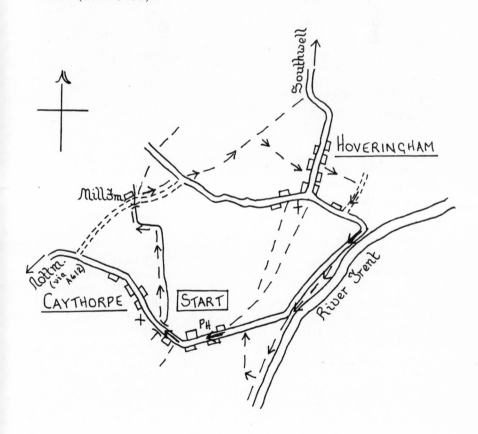

*Some of the most delightful walks in Nottinghamshire – and some of the easiest –*
*follow the banks of the 'smug and silver' Trent, and this walk is typical. Level walking*
*all the way, with a good balance between well cultivated arable fields and pleasant*
*riverside meadows. An added attraction on the route is the charming village of*
*Hoveringham where, depending on the time of day, you may be able to obtain liquid*
*refreshment.*

## The Walk

Follow the village road in the direction of Lowdham, leaving by a waymarked footpath on the right, beside the bridge over the Dover Beck.
Follow the beckside faithfully, for much of the way keeping to the top
of the floodbank. Cross a stile and continue over a field, still beside
the beck, to reach and cross a well constructed stile. Go over the
succeeding field to reach a farm lane and turn right, to Mill Farm. Pass
through the farm grounds, crossing the beck, here the mill stream, by
a footbridge (or, if you like, via the ford). Keep to the waymarked route,
turning left from the farm lane, into the fields, then right to follow the
hedge and ditch. A good path leads all the way to the Hoveringham –
Gonalston road, which is met directly beneath a power line.

Cross the road and continue, still beside the hedge and ditch, but
now following a farm track. After some distance, this reverts to a
footpath, and you pass a solitary oak tree on your left. A little further
on, turn right and descend carefully by the steps provided to cross the
ditch by a plank bridge, then follow the path beside the hedge over
two fields and a stream to continue past the cricket field – watching
out, if they are playing, for any six-shots! A welcome bonus here, in
the summer months, is that the Reindeer Inn backs onto the cricket
ground and, if a game is in progress, the Boundary Bar may be open,
in which case you can sit and slake your thirst, while watching.

Join the road and turn left through Hoveringham village, leaving
again by a waymarked path on the right, opposite the post office. A
somewhat overgrown way leads through a small wood and over a
stream (the Causeway Dyke) into a field. Continue alongside the hedge
to the top of the field and turn right, following the hedge round to a
stile – an unusual one this, as the footboard slopes at a 45° angle!
Turn left over the stile and follow the hedge to another stile. Cross,
and turn right along Lodgefield Lane to the road and turn left,
following the road round to the riverside. Keep to the riverside road
as far as the parking area, leaving the road here, by the towpath gate,
to follow the riverside path upstream. Cross a stile and keep on, with
a hedge parallel on your right. Towards the overhead telephone lines,
bear right to turn around the angle of the hedge and reach a stile.
Cross, and follow a short enclosed length of path to the field, then
turn right along the field side to reach the road. Turn left for the inn.

# Flintham

**21**

## The Boot and Shoe

An arched passageway leading into the car park suggests that this might once have served as a coaching inn, and, although it was never on any official routes, the landlord confirms that some coaches called here. Of more recent interest, though, is the popularity of this hostelry with wartime aircrew from the nearby airfields at Syerston and Newton. While relaxing in the lounge of this quiet village inn, it is not difficult to picture the scene in more turbulent times, with the off-duty crews gathered around the bar. The heroes of yesteryear have moved on, but the memorabilia remains as a lasting memento. There are pictures of once familiar aircraft and the citation of Flight Lieutenant Reade VC who, as well as Wing Commander Guy Gibson, of Dam-Busters fame, was once a patron of the inn. But the battles of more recent years are not forgotten and you will see also an unusual bell, fashioned from a shell-case, recalling the Falklands campaign. Other distinctive features of this interesting inn include a masonry beehive in the car park, and some distinctive herringbone brickwork.

The Boot and Shoe is a Home Brewery house, and the ales include Theakston XB, as well as Home Mild and Bitter. The speciality draught cider is Scrumpy Jack. Food is available daily, both lunchtimes and evenings, with a set lunch, to order only, on Sundays. The range of delicacies on offer includes rump steak, gammon steak, fillet of plaice and home-made drover's pie. Or you can settle for a simpler snack from the range of rolls and sandwiches.

There is a pleasant beer garden and children's play area outside. Well behaved dogs are welcome.

Telephone: Newark (0636) 525246.

*How to get there:* Flintham lies just to the east of the A46 Fosse Way, 10 miles south west of Newark, the inn being situated in the centre of the village.

*Parking:* There is an enclosed car park directly behind the inn, accessed through an archway between the buildings, where you may park while you go on your walk.

*Public transport:* Lincolnshire Road Car buses (Newark to Bingham service) call here and Newark to Nottingham buses connect with the village lane at the Fosse Way (¾ mile).

*Length of the walk:* 5 miles (shorter alternative 2¼ miles). Maps: OS Landranger series 129 Nottingham and Loughborough, Pathfinder series SK 64/74 Carlton and Elston (GR 742460).

*We follow quiet fields to Syerston village, an oasis of calm, separated from the airfield of the same name by the busy Fosse Way. Then on to the outskirts of Sibthorpe, another tiny, mainly agricultural community, from whence we return to Flintham along peaceful lanes and bridleways. The once busy wartime skies are quiet now and you are unlikely to encounter anything more aggressive in the aeronautical line than a glider or two.*

**The Walk**

Turn right out of the inn and follow the main street, turning at the bend onto Inholms Road. Beyond the next bend, take a waymarked metalled track on the right, beside the houses. On reaching a high gate, turn right and follow the path skirting a fenced enclosure (sewage works). Cross a footbridge and continue ahead on the left of the hedge. At the top of the rise, pass through a gap in the hedge and continue, now on the right of the hedge.

At an enclosed track (Longhedge Lane), turn right for a short way, then left again, continuing over the fields and aiming to the right of Syerston church. Briefly enter the grounds of a private house (the waymarked path goes that way), following the hedge on your left, to reach the road, and there turn right. As you turn onto the road you

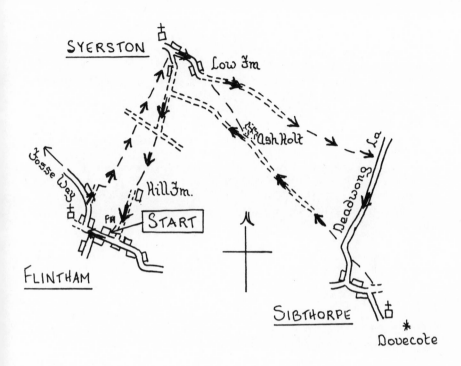

SYERSTON

Low Frm

Ash Holt

Fosse Way

Deadwong La

Hill 3m.

FM

START

FLINTHAM

SIBTHORPE

Dovecote

will note that the way here branches.

*For the shorter walk,* take the right fork (Hawksworth Lane). This connects with the return route of the longer walk. Follow the directions in the final paragraph.

*For the main walk,* take the left fork and follow Moor Lane through the village and on, past Low Farm, to open country. The scene now opens out, with wide views across the Vale of Belvoir.

Where the lane ends, continue ahead, now on a field path alongside a dike, to reach a road and turn right. Follow this quiet unfenced country road (with the delightful name of Deadwong Lane) as far as the next bend. There is a proliferation of power lines in this area, and you will find yourself faced, apparently, by an army of giants. But don't be scared, they are only electricity pylons and you will soon put them behind you, unless, of course, you wish to visit the village of Sibthorpe, now visible ahead. It is off our route, and is not a big village, but it is distinguished as having a fine dovecote, and a massive yew hedge around the church.

Leave Deadwong Lane on the bend, under the power line. Ignore the farm track on the left of the field here, and stick strictly to the line indicated by the guide post. This crosses a very large field and the path may not be evident on the ground. But you should be able to make out the houses of Syerston in the far distance, and this is the direction to make for, and an intermediate guide post in the middle distance. On reaching the guide post, cross over the adjacent stream and join a clear track way.

The track leads into a green lane beside a small wood, Ash Holt. Continue on along the lane, now bypassing Syerston village and, on reaching a T junction, turn left.

Follow this green lane away from Syerston. At the next T junction (Longhedge Lane), turn right and left again, now going along a field path. After passing Hill Farm the path develops into a farm lane, Woods Lane, which is followed all the way through to Flintham. Turn right for the inn.

# **Wilford**
## The Ferry Inn

There is no ferry at Wilford these days – and no ford either, for that matter – but the Ferry Inn flourishes. A charming old white-painted village inn, said to have been built originally as a coffee house in the late 15th century, the Ferry is something of an anomaly, situated as it is within the boundary of the City of Nottingham. A more macabre twist in the tale of this intriguing inn is the fact that the building once served as a mortuary for people drowned in the river, and one of the seats still in use today is claimed to have been used as the slab on which the bodies were laid out.

The Ferry belongs to Premier House and the facilities include a well patronised and excellent dining area, which consists of a fascinating collection of interconnecting rooms with ancient beams and timbers, horse brasses, pistols and warming pans, and is separate from the busy lounge.

Food is available at lunchtimes and in the evenings, seven days a week, and you will be able to choose from a wide selection of meals and bar snacks, the menu being displayed on a large blackboard behind the servery – and the hot roast beef cob with chips is something else! Children's portions are also available. Both

Shipstone's and Tetley Bitter are on offer, as is draught cider. The inn has a garden area and a no smoking zone, and dogs are welcome, but only in the garden. The proprietor does not favour visitors consuming their own food here, but then, there is plenty of choice on the menu.

Telephone: Nottingham (0602) 811441.

*How to get there:* The Ferry Inn can be approached on foot, over the Wilford former toll bridge from Riverside Way, in the Meadows area of the city. The only access by road is via Wilford crossroads on the B679 road between West Bridgford and Clifton.

*Parking:* Apart from the inn car park, there is ample parking space alongside the Wilford Bridge approach road.

*Public transport:* The route is well served by Nottingham City Transport. The Wilford Village service passes the inn, and numerous routes connect with various points along the way.

*Length of the walk:* 5½ miles. Maps: OS Landranger series 129 Nottingham and Loughborough, Pathfinder series SK 43/53 Long Eaton, Estate Publications Red Book – Nottingham (GR 568378).

*Everybody has heard of the river Trent, few know the river Leen. Yet this humble little waterway has a far sounder claim to the title of Nottingham's river than has the more illustrious Trent. For in former times, when the ancient town was confined to the high ground around the Castle and Lace Market, the Trent was a mile distant, beyond the meadows and marshes to the south. This walk visits both rivers, and an even humbler tributary, the Tinker's Leen. But most of the time is spent along the towpath of the Nottingham Canal.*

*This is an urban walk, beside urban waterways. For much of the way we walk in the shadow of ancient factories and warehouses. Yet even in the heart of this great city, it is easy to forget the close proximity of 20th century industry and commerce, in the company of quiet anglers and slow-moving water traffic.*

**The Walk**

Follow the road north from the inn to reach and cross Wilford Bridge. No toll is exacted these days, and the bridge is closed to vehicular traffic, but the toll house is still there, with its table of charges displayed over the door. We used to call it the 'Ha'penny Bridge', because that was the charge for pedestrians 'when I were a lad'.

Turn left over the bridge, crossing Riverside Way and cutting through to Robin Hood Way, the Meadows Estate peripheral road. After passing to the rear of Wickes store, cut through onto Queen's Drive and cross over to reach Crossgate Drive. Pass between a

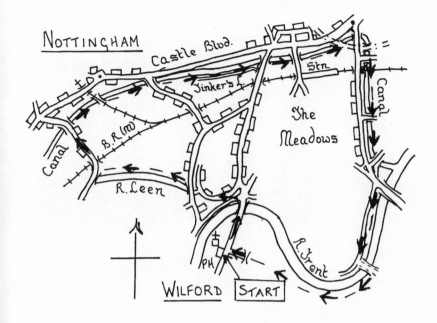

shrubbery and a culvert on the corner of Crossgate Drive to join a cycle way. The culvert, to the left of the paved path, is the river Leen, enclosed here as a safety measure, because the river disappears underground at this point, not to resurface until reaching its outflow into the Trent. The Leen has been sadly used over the years, pushed out of sight, diverted from its true course, polluted and forgotten. Now, something at least has been done to restore this little river's self-esteem and, from close by Crossgate Drive to Lenton Lane, the stream once more flows between grass banks.

Follow the cycle track through to Lenton Lane, ignoring side turnings and keeping in close contact with the Leen. Central Television's studios are a prominent landmark ahead and to the left.

Turn right at Lenton Lane, crosssing the railway and following the road until you reach the canal bridge. Cross the road and join the towpath, turning right immediately to pass under the road. A very pleasant canalside walk follows, the waterway busy with canal boats, fishermen and waterfowl. As you approach the Castle Marina you will have a good view of Nottingham Castle, directly ahead atop its sandstone rock.

Past the Marina a graceful footbridge is crossed, and the canal path passes close by the Castle Park retail estate. Despite the close

proximity of busy Castle Boulevard, the next section of the canal retains a semi-rural atmosphere. The Tinker's Leen bears company with the canal here, struggling bravely against adversity to assert itself. Attempts have been made to improve this tiny waterway which, in the past, has been treated even more harshly than the Leen. But it is an ongoing task, and much still remains to be done.

The canal passes beneath Wilford Road, close by the Navigation Inn and a working lock. Then on past the Canal Museum, well worth visiting but, to do so, you will need to ascend to Carrington Street and walk round onto Canal Street, there being no direct route over the canal here.

Go under Carrington Street, passing the Crown Court on your left. There is a good view to the left here of the old city area on the hilltop, with St Mary's parish church and the Lace Centre (formerly the Unitarian chapel) prominent.

After crossing Trent Street, a sterner section of canal ensues, as we pass between tall old buildings and the now-disused railway viaduct. Pass under London Road and turn right with the canal before crossing, with the towpath, to the eastern bank of the canal.

The canal now follows London Road, passing beneath the railway. Among the buildings visible along the road, look out for the especially fine façade of the Hicking Pentecost building. After crossing Cattle Market Road and Meadow Lane, the canal swings left to enter the

92

Turney's Quay Estate, and further progress along the towpath is barred by a gated fence.

Ascend the stairway left to reach the estate, following the road round to reach and cross a footbridge over the canal. Turn left again along the estate road, passing Turney's Court – formerly a leather works, but now converted to residential use – and continuing along towards the end of the road, where a twitchell on the right will lead you out to the riverside, opposite the Forest football ground, Rushcliffe Council's offices, and a row of boat clubhouses.

Turn right, following the riverside path under Trent Bridge, and noting the flood levels cut into the wall as you emerge on the far side. The large building over the river here is County Hall, the Nottinghamshire County Council offices. Continue on along the riverside, noting the imposing entrance to the memorial gardens, which you may consider worth visiting (and where toilets are available).

Cross the river by the Suspension Bridge, turning right to rejoin the riverside path. Follow an enclosed way between the flood wall and the river, passing the Becket Upper School and the Rivermead flats complex. On reaching the fields, ascend to the top of the floodbank and follow the metalled path, enjoying the excellent views across a broad sweep of the river.

After passing the Wilford Meadows school and under a redundant railway bridge, re-ascend to the top of the floodbank, passing the Coronation Pond on your right to reach the Ferry Inn.

# 23 **Beeston**
## The Boat and Horses Inn

The Boat and Horses is a busy and spacious 'local' on the Beeston Rylands residential estate, and its outward appearance blends in with its surroundings. This is perhaps surprising, because the inn was built ahead of the estate, in the 19th century, at which time most of the surrounding farmland belonged to the Prince of Wales, a frequent visitor to this area. The name of the house reflects the fact that the Nottingham and Beeston Canal is close by.

The inn belongs to the Home Brewery (Scottish and Newcastle), and hand-pulled real ales include Home Mild and Bitter, Theakston XB, No 3 and Scotch Bitter, with Strongbow and Woodpecker for the cider drinker. Meals and bar snacks are provided every lunchtime from Monday to Friday, the speciality here being home-made curry, and the tender, hot beef sandwiches would bring a smile to anyone's face! The inn has a beer garden and children's play area, as well as a function room. Dogs, however, are not encouraged.

Telephone: Nottingham (0602) 258589.

*How to get there:* From Beeston town centre and the Beeston bypass,

94

follow Station Road and Meadow Road, turning right at the end along Canal Side. Trent Road is some way along on your right, and the inn is likewise a short distance along Trent Road, on the right.

*Parking:* You may leave your car in the spacious pub car park as you wish. But there is ample alternative parking space hereabouts – along Canal Side or, if you opt to follow the walk from Attenborough, in the Nature Reserve car park.

*Public transport:* There are buses from Broad Marsh, Nottingham (Barton). British Rail Nottingham – Derby service calls at Beeston (½ mile) and Attenborough (¼ mile from the Nature Reserve).

*Length of the walk:* 3½ miles. Maps: OS Landranger series 129 Nottingham and Loughborough, Pathfinder series SK 43/53 Long Eaton (GR 537355).

*Our walk begins and ends beside the Beeston Canal and Weir, and the riverside;
in between we follow a circular route around the Attenborough Nature Reserve.
Much of the Trent Valley has been subjected to exploitation by the gravel companies
and it might be supposed that, as a result, vast areas have been laid waste. But nothing
could be further from the truth. The former gravel pits at Holme Pierrepont have
been remodelled into the National Water Sports Centre and Country Park. Those at
Attenborough have been largely left to the healing hand of nature, to become a most
excellent Nature Reserve, rich in wild fowl and popular with visitors from miles
around.*

## The Walk

From the inn, follow Trent Road down to Canal Side and turn right.
As you leave the inn you will be able to see, away over the river, the
woods of Clifton Grove, and Clifton Hall and church. Follow the canal
as far as Beeston Lock and the riverside marina, full of life, with a
plenitude of boats, and a tea and coffee shop where you can obtain
refreshments (including food on the inn's non-catering days) either on
the outward or the return journey.

On reaching a broad path on the right, leave the riverside and enter
the Attenborough Nature Reserve. Bear left at the railway, walking
through a wild wonderland of trees, shrubs and water. Where the path
branches by the gravel works, bear right and cross a gracefully arched
footbridge over a branch of the pits and continue forward until you
emerge onto a road (The Strand) in the village. Attenborough is
virtually an island today, surrounded on three sides by the waters of
the Nature Reserve and on the fourth by the railway. The village has
passed into history as the home of Henry Ireton, the lieutenant of
Oliver Cromwell who, we are told, stabled his horses in the nave of
Attenborough church.

Turn left at the end of the sports field, keeping to the right as you
pass through the car park. Cross another arched footbridge. This end
of the Nature Reserve is the most popular with visitors – and with the
wildfowl, which know when they are on a winner, foodwise! You will
see mallard here in abundance, and Canada geese, as well as water
hens, although these last tend to be more solitary in their habits. These
varieties are just a few of the many types of wildlife to be spotted here
by the diligent observer.

Turn left on reaching the river, almost opposite Barton Island, and
follow the riverside back to Beeston Lock, the canal and the inn,
enjoying as you go the wide views over the broad waterway to Brands
Hill and Clifton Cliff.

# 24 Cotgrave
## The Manvers Arms

Cotgrave has seen many changes in my own lifetime. The colliery –
now closed down – was sunk since the last war, and many of the
miners came here from the north east. You will, without doubt, hear
echoes of Tyneside in the accents here. But the presence on its door-
step of this once proud pit and its loyal workforce has not destroyed
the essentially rural character of the village and its surroundings.

An imposing inn – as befits a house dedicated to one of the
county's most celebrated titled families – the Manvers stands in the
very centre of the old village. Three roads meet here, the respective
junctions being occupied by the three most important buildings in any
community – the church, the pub, and the post office!

Built about 1725, the Manvers (then the Black Lion) was formerly a
coaching inn, and the ancient timbers and bare brickwork in the
lounge area, itself converted from the previous living accommodation,
serve to reflect the impression of great age.

A Greenalls/Shipstone's house, the real ales here include both
Shipstone's and Tetley, and Strongbow Cider is also available. Food
is available every day from 12 noon until 2.30 pm, and the varied
menu inludes home-made pies and pastries – the speciality here – as

97

well as chicken and seafood items, cheese toasties, pizzas, not to mention the ever-popular assortment of sausage, egg, burger, beans and chip dishes. There is a special children's menu too. On top of all this, there are daily specials, and you can also obtain a traditional Sunday lunch.

There is a beer garden and children's area, where you may, if food is not available, eat your own snap. Well behaved dogs are welcome.

Telephone: Nottingham (0602) 892293.

*How to get there:* Cotgrave can be reached from the A606 (Nottingham/ Melton) road, at Plumtree, from the A52 (Nottingham/Grantham) road at Holme House, near Radcliffe, or from the A46 (Fosse Way, Leicester/ Newark) road, between Saxondale and Widmerpool. The Manvers Arms is in the middle of the village, on the junction of the three principal approach roads.

*Parking:* You are welcome to use the inn's own car park, if using the facilities, but some roadside parking is also possible, with care, on some of the village roads.

*Public transport:* Buses run from Nottingham (Barton's Redmile and Stathern service).

*Length of the walk:* 6¼ miles. Maps: OS Landranger series 129 Nottingham and Loughborough, Pathfinder series SK 63/73 Radcliffe on Trent (GR 645354).

*Crossing the fields to the neighbouring village of Tollerton and following the quiet road through this unspoilt village, we make our way, again by field paths and the Polser Brook, to the attractive residential village of Normanton on the Wolds; then to the tiny farming community of Clipston on the Wolds and back to Cotgrave, enjoying wide views along the way over Nottingham and the Trent Valley.*

**The Walk**

Cross the Plumtree Road and follow Church Lane (beside the parish church), bearing right onto the waymarked path for Tollerton. Cross a stile onto the fields and turn left, over the field and on along an enclosed track, turning off left through a gap to continue, still in the same direction, on the left of the hedge. Past a sewage works, turn left at the service road and, immediately, right again.

Still following the hedge-side, waymarked with a 'Grantham Canal Circular Walks' marker; after a double bend in the hedge, turn right over a stile and cross the next field diagonally, heading directly for a tall tree. Pass through the hedge and by the tree, crossing over a series

98

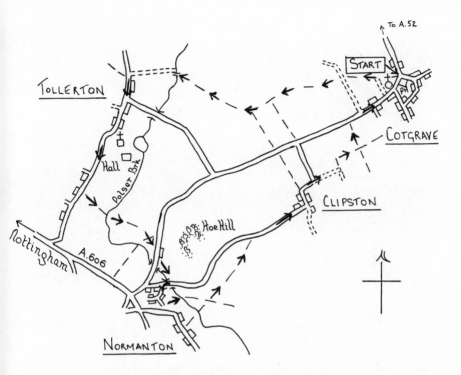

of large arable fields, and bearing right a smidgin in the third field to reach and cross a plank bridge and meet a farm track.

Cross the track and keep straight on towards distant barn-type structures. Passing through a hedge, turn left to follow the perimeter of the field round to a stout footbridge. Cross over, and follow the track all the way through to Tollerton village, where you turn left.

Tollerton still manages to retain the atmosphere of a traditional agricultural community. Small as it is, there is no lack of interesting buildings here, including the North End Cottages, a unique gatehouse, a fine parish church, and an ancient manor house. The Hall – its old name of Roclaveston Manor points out the tortuous derivation of the village name of Tollerton – served as a prisoner of war camp (one of my most vivid memories is of a weekend spent camping at Hall Farm just after the war, when we fraternised with our country's erstwhile enemies!). Today it is the offices of an insurance company.

Follow the road through the village. A seat beside the war memorial, opposite the church entrance, offers an excellent opportunity for a rest, before continuing round the double bend and on up the hill to Hall Farm. There is a pavement on the left of the road, all the way

through the village, but it runs out at the farm entrance and, for safety, you should cross over here, to use the pavement on the other side, alongside the more modern houses.

A little way on beyond Hall Farm, a stile leads off left. Cross this and follow the field's edge down the field and around the end to reach and cross a nice solid footbridge over the Polser Brook. Continue on to the left of a residual hedge, heading directly towards Hoe Hill Wood. Towards the end of the field, pass through the gap to the opposite side of the hedge.

The correct route here crosses the field diagonally in the direction of Hoe Hill Cottage – the white cottage visible across the field. In practice, you are unlikely to find a trodden path here, despite the guide post at the road-end, and you will surely be excused for following the hedge down to the road, where a second path emerges onto the road, having crossed the field from the other corner.

The way continues via a footpath in the field to the right of Hoe Hill Cottage. Follow the path round beside the brook, crossing a footbridge to reach Clipston Lane and a seat. Follow the road right, turning left almost immediately into The Leys, an estate of modern houses. Follow the houses round on your left, leaving the estate by a footpath between numbers 6 and 7, lined on either side by tall cupressus hedges. The way crosses a splendid footbridge after which it branches. Take the left fork, crossing the stile directly in front. A delightfully adventurous path leads back over the brook and onto pasture land, skirting around Normanton on the Wolds village.

Keep towards the right of the field, with hawthorns on your right, following a faintly defined path. Turn left onto a crossing path from Normanton, then on over a farm lane and three fields to reach the road (Clipston Lane). There are superb views from this field path over to the left, across the Trent Valley and the city of Nottingham. Cross the stile to join the road and turn right to reach Clipston village. Cotgrave Forest – another good venue for a ramble – will be seen over to your right from the lane here.

Follow the road through the little village, leaving on the third bend to follow a broad wooded track beside Boot Pit Plantation. Emerging from the wood, continue between an avenue of trees, with Cotgrave village and pit visible ahead. Turn left at the end of the trees, following the nearside of the hedge, then turn right with the path over a shallow ditch and continue on the right of the hedge in front. Turn left at a gap in the hedge (a path crosses from the right here) and cross straight down the field to the Plumtree Road. Turn right now and follow the road back into Cotgrave.

# 25 Colston Bassett
## The Martins Arms

Built about 300 years ago as a farmhouse on the Colston Bassett Estate, the Martins Arms boasts among its antiquities a Jacobean fireplace – and the ghost of a Lady in Grey. As you might expect, for this is Belvoir Hunt country, the lounge is decorated with hunting scenes. And coal and log fires add a cheerful winter note.

The Martins is a freehouse with a wide selection of real ales, Marston's Traditional, Pedigree, Bateman XB and XXXB, Bass, Speckled Hen, Abbott Ale, Maclay 80/- Export and Fuller's London Pride. Not to mention Strongbow Draught Cider. Bar meals and snacks, and a full dining room menu, are available every lunchtime, and in the evenings from Tuesday to Saturday. This is the Vale of Belvoir and, naturally, the bill of fare includes both Stilton cheese and Melton Mowbray pies. You may choose from a selection of rolls and sandwiches, and specialities include such exotica as parsnip and onion soup, medallions of monkfish, and roast mallard. It is a boast of the house that all the food is fresh (no microwaves or freezers) and appropriate dishes are cooked on a smoked charcoal grill.

The inn has a most attractive garden area, popular with children. Telephone: Bingham (0949) 81361.

*How to get there:* From the A46 Fosse Way (Leicester to Newark) turn east, south of Radcliffe, onto the Cotgrave to Colston Bassett road. Turn right at the village cross (a National Trust property) and the inn is on your right.

*Parking:* There is no objection to walking patrons parking in the pub car park for the duration.

*Public transport:* Buses between Nottingham and Long Clawson (Barton) call at Colston Bassett.

*Length of the walk:* 5 miles. Maps: OS Landranger series 129 Nottingham and Loughborough, Pathfinder series SK 63/73 Radcliffe on Trent (GR 698331).

*Colston Bassett is a particularly attractive and unspoilt village in the Vale of Belvoir, which still retains its traditional rural charm. The old village church of St Mary, which will be visited on this walk, was made redundant 100 years ago, when*

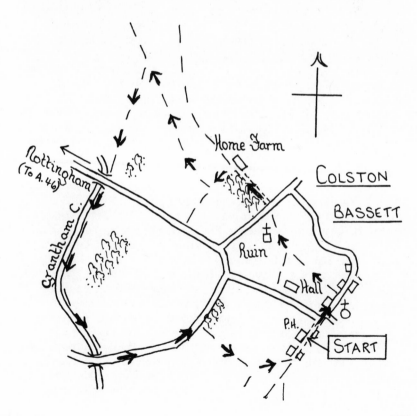

*an impressive replacement was built in the centre of the village, and the village cross, a few yards from the inn, is one of the National Trust's only three properties in the county.*

### The Walk

Follow School Lane down to the cross and continue along the village street, past the church. Leave by a footpath on the left leading into parkland. Head slightly right, making for a clump of trees behind which (depending on the season) the tower of the old church may be visible. Beyond the trees, bear left a little to pass behind the little sports pavilion, then right again to reach a farm gate and a track leading past the old church.

The sad old creeper-covered ruins of the ancient church occupy a lovely site on the top of the rise. You are advised, for safety reasons, not to enter the building, but the grounds themselves are worth visiting to see the remains of this once beautiful house of God.

Cross the road and follow a metalled farm road to Home Farm. Pass to the left of the buildings, entering the field and turning left down the centre. As you near the bottom of the field bear right, to reach a metal farm gate. Pass through and turn right, following the hedge and ditch.

After passing under a power line cross a stile and the ensuing two fields, adopting the Cropwell Bishop church tower as a useful waymark ahead. In the third field bear left to reach and follow the left-side fence down to a stile in the bottom corner. Cross the next field, also diagonally, and again to a stile in the bottom corner – but resist the temptation to cross this stile. Instead, turn your back on it, and on Cropwell Bishop, and follow a new path, with the hedge on your right. At the end of the field, cross a solid footbridge and then go over the middle of the next field, thence again on the left of the hedge beside two successive fields to reach the road. At the appropriate times of year, keep your ears peeled in this area for skylarks and, in the nearby woods, woodpeckers.

Cross the road and join the canal towpath. The Grantham Canal has been out of use for many years and this stretch is low on water, but it still provides a peaceful and popular stroll.

At Spencer's Bridge leave the canal, turning left along the road. Continue, crossing a stream and going on until you reach a footpath sign beside a wood. Follow a good farm track from here to its end at a farm gate. Bear right in the field to reach and cross the river Smite, then bear left over the 'ridge and furrow', making for a cream-coloured cottage, and ignoring a prominent footpath sign some distance to its right. A stile directly on the right of the cottage gives cleaner – and nearer – access to School Lane, and a short easy stroll back to the inn.

# 26 Kinoulton
## The Nevile Arms

Kinoulton stands on the edge of the Vale of Belvoir; a typical South Nottinghamshire village of mellow red brick and pantiles, with its complement of more modern housing. The Nevile fits precisely into neither category; rather, it is an agreeable compromise between the two, a pleasant and welcoming 'Kimberley' house at the eastern end of the main street. The lounge is recommended for its tasteful decor and welcoming atmosphere. There are two traditional open fireplaces, one at either end of the room, the wall furnishings include a number of period pictures and a pendulum wall-clock, a group of china figures occupy a shelf behind the tastefully panelled bar counter, and elsewhere you will see collections of copper kettles and pans.

The speciality ale here is Kimberley Classic and both Strongbow and Blackthorn Cider are available on draught. Hot meals are provided lunchtimes and evenings, every day from Tuesday to Saturday, and the range is impressive. There is a selection of steak, fish and vegetarian platters to tempt your taste buds, as well as chef's specials, and 'lunchtime quickies'. Snacks include an assortment of cold cobs and sandwiches. The chef takes a well-earned break on Sunday and Monday, but the cobs and sandwiches are still available and are a meal in themselves.

The lounge is a non-smoking area. There is an outside children's area and beer garden. And dogs are welcome inside, but not, please, in the garden. Walkers are particularly welcome, but it might be tempting providence if you enter the carpeted lounge without first removing muddy boots. Size of party is no deterrent, but it would be appreciated if leaders of large groups could give prior notice.

Telephone: Bingham (0949) 81236.

*How to get there:* Kinoulton lies to the east of the A46 (Fosse Way) and north of the A606 Nottingham to Melton Mowbray road. The most direct access is via the unclassified road from Widmerpool, which crosses both of these roads.

*Parking:* For the duration of your walk and your visit, you may use the inn's own car park.

*Public transport:* Barton's Nottingham to Melton bus service serves Kinoulton.

*Length of the walk:* 4¼ miles. Maps: OS Landranger series 129 Nottingham and Loughborough, Pathfinder series SK 63/73 Radcliffe on Trent (GR 681310).

*The linear village of Kinoulton spans the disused Grantham Canal, on the very rim of the Vale of Belvoir, the home of the matchless Stilton cheese. The land to the east is relatively flat, but we go to the slightly higher ground to the west, where a surprisingly modest elevation opens up an incredibly wide view over the Vale.*

## The Walk

Follow Owthorpe Road north from the inn, keeping straight ahead where the road branches and taking the minor road towards the hamlet of Owthorpe. On reaching the canal turn left, following the green towpath along the nearside of the waterway. Although out of use for many years, and now unnavigable, there is still plenty of water in this first short stretch of the canal, and no lack of waterfowl, swans, mallard and coot.

Continue on the towpath around the right angled bend of Devil's Elbow to reach and cross a bridge. Head away from the canal now, following a farm lane between an avenue of Lombardy poplars. Pass the stern buildings of Vimy Ridge Farm and continue ahead, now following a green field track, with the woodlands of Kinoulton Gorse

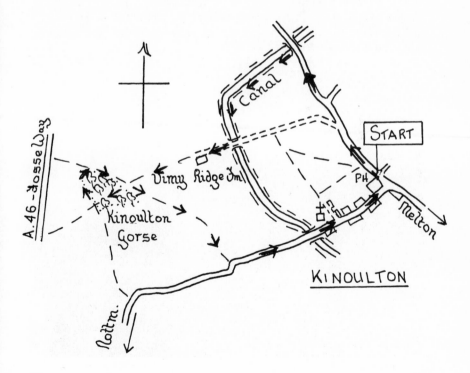

directly ahead. This is a good place to pause and turn around, to enjoy the magnificent view over the Vale of Belvoir. Belvoir Castle, a home of the Duke of Rutland, should be discernible on the skyline, at the left hand end of a wooded ridge, and to the right of the tower silo at Vimy Ridge Farm.

On reaching the wood, continue straight ahead, following a footpath through the wood. At the far side – and now within sight of the Roman Fosse Way – turn right to follow the footpath around three sides of the wood. Look out for the sad remains of an old farm cart and an abandoned item of farm machinery, buried in the brambles and undergrowth.

Back on the Kinoulton side of the wood, recross the Vimy Ridge track, still keeping to the left of the wood. Beyond the next hedge and just a short distance further on, bear left, following the side of the field. Initially the field boundary is recognisable only from the presence of undergrowth, but the hedge develops as you proceed down the field in the direction of Kinoulton. The path is depicted on the map as following the left hand side of the hedge, but a clearer and easier track follows the right hand side, and this appears to be the route generally favoured by strollers and riders.

Cross an open field and continue beside the hedge to reach the road, at the western end of the village. Follow the village road past the canal, and the red-brick village church, back to the inn.

# 27 Gotham
## The Sun Inn

Gotham is a large unpretentious village whose economy has traditionally rested largely on the mining of gypsum, an occupation which has now almost died out, although British Gypsum still has considerable interests hereabouts. But the village should not be regarded as commonplace. It was here, in the Middle Ages, that the legend was born of the 'Wise Men of Gotham' – those astute individuals who, to deter the King from making a home in the vicinity (and, presumably, saddling the villagers with its upkeep), contrived, by various acts of foolishness, to convince the royal emissaries that this would not, after all, be the best place for His Majesty to set up house.

The Sun is a pleasant and friendly village inn, situated at the heart of this interesting old village. An Everards house, the selection of real ales includes Beacon Bitter, Tiger Best and Old Original. Guest ales are a feature here, and draught cider is also available. There is a good and varied menu, chalked up on a blackboard in the lounge. I selected a delicious portion of plaice in breadcrumbs, but alternatives on offer include scampi, chicken and lasagne, all with the option of either chips or new potatoes. Sunday specials include roast beef or lamb, with soup or alternative starter, a selection of desserts, and coffee. Ploughman's lunch is also provided.

The inn possesses a spacious beamed lounge and a comfortable bar room. A garden area is provided for the children, and those preferring fresh air. Dogs are welcome outside. Customers may consume their own food in the garden area, but it would be courteous to verify this with the landlord before doing so.

Telephone: Nottingham (0602) 830484.

*How to get there:* Gotham is situated about 7 miles south of Nottingham on the unclassified road betwen Clifton and East Leake. The Sun is one of four inns serving this flourishing village, and stands in the little village square, directly opposite the parish church of St Lawrence.

*Parking:* The inn has its own car park, and a few spaces are also available in the public square, alongside the church wall.

*Public transport:* Gotham is served by a regular bus service (Nottingham City Transport/South Notts) between Nottingham and Loughborough.

*Length of the walk:* 3½ miles. Maps: OS Landranger series 129 Nottingham and Loughborough, Pathfinder series SK 42/52 Loughborough North and Castle Donington, and SK 43/53 Long Eaton (GR 536302).

*The village sits in a crescent of low hills which provide a wealth of excellent walks, such as this one, along well defined fieldpaths and bridleways.*

## The Walk

Leaving the village square, follow the Leake Road south, past the church and on to the end of the village. Bear right at the end of the houses, following unmetalled Hill Road up towards the gypsum workings. Pass around the end of a gate, continuing along the same track and crossing the route of a former mineral line and thence on along a narrower path to reach a handgate on the left. Through this gate, follow the right hand side of the field steeply uphill beside a wood.

At the top of the hill the ground levels off and a path is met, coming along the ridge from the left to pass through a handgate. Through the gate turn right, passing Cuckoo Bush Wood and heading for Cuckoo Bush Farm. It was here that those wise men of yesteryear achieved particular fame when they attempted to fence in a cuckoo, 'so that he

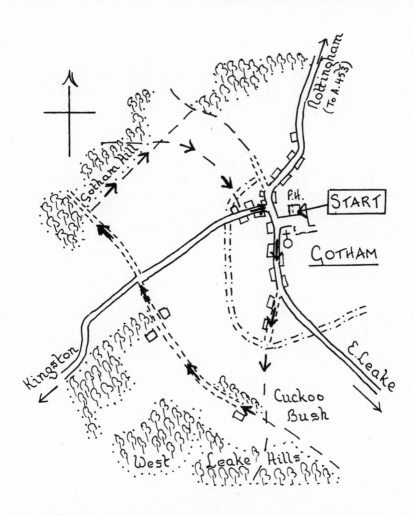

would sing to them all the year round'.

Beyond the farm the path develops into a firmer track and the scene broadens out. A wide area of South Nottinghamshire comes into view, extending over Gotham to the outskirts of Nottingham, and over to the pit-head gear of Cotgrave; and to the west over the Leicestershire borderland, with a glimpse of the cooling towers of Ratcliffe on Soar Power Station.

Cross the Kingston road and continue straight ahead, climbing steeply up to Stonepit Wood and Cottager's Hill. A rustic seat here offers the welcome opportunity to pause for a while and enjoy the views.

Follow the hilltop footpath beside Gotham Hill Wood. At the end of this first very long field, pass through a field gate and continue on to meet a path coming in through the woods on the left, from Thrumpton. Bear right, making for the right hand end of a wood which can be seen peeping over the crest of the hill, and arrive at a stile beside a gate. Beyond the stile, contour around the hill and wood to reach a stile on your right, which cross, and follow the ensuing field path down the left side of the next field to cross the former mineral line.

Follow the schoolhouse drive past the primary school, to reach the road. Turn left, then right at the next junction, to arrive back at the village square.

## Hickling
# The Plough

(28)

Idyllically situated adjacent to a basin on the disused Grantham Canal, on the edge of the Vale of Belvoir, the interior of the Plough reflects both the customs of canal life and the hunting tradition of the Leicestershire border. The tiny lounge contains a number of items of canal boat memorabilia, prettily decorated jugs and the like, while hunting pictures and a hunting horn – along with other brass and copperware – decorate the cosy snug, with its brick chimney breast, welcoming open fire in winter, and traditional oak beams. We are told that the beer used to be brought up from the cellar in jugs, to be sent around to the fishermen on the canal basin.

The inn belongs to Younger/Home Brewery, and real ales include Theakston XB and Old Peculier. The draught cider here is Dry Blackthorn. Food is provided every lunchtime, and evenings too, except Tuesday evening. The menu is changed regularly, with specials being displayed on the blackboards. A particularly popular item is rack of ribs, or you may wish to try Yorkshire pudding, with a choice of several different fillings. Otherwise you may choose from a range of salads, sausage dishes, pork burgers and jacket potatoes. Then again, there is a different, but full, evening meal menu.

There is a combined beer garden/children's area, and also a family room, and well behaved dogs are welcome, but only if kept on a lead.
Telephone: Melton Mowbray (0664) 822225.

*How to get there:* From the A606 (Nottingham/Melton) road, turn north east at Hickling Pastures, 1 mile east of the Widmerpool roundabout on the A46 Fosse Way, to bring you to Hickling village. Turn left and the Plough is at the end of the village, opposite the canal basin.

*Parking:* There is adequate parking behind the inn, but let a member of staff know if you intend to leave your vehicle there while you walk.

*Public transport:* There are buses from Nottingham and Melton (Barton).

*Length of the walk:* 4¾ miles. Maps: OS Landranger series 129 Nottingham and Loughborough, Pathfinder series SK 62/72 Scalford and Nether Broughton (GR 691295).

*Nottinghamshire boasts no great hills. But those hills we do have – in many cases – afford distant prospects quite on a par with anything offered by some of the grander belvederes. One such is Hickling Standard. Although at the modest altitude of 344 ft, we defy anyone to stand on this breezy hilltop, or on the nearby quiet country lane, on a clear and bright day, and not be charmed by the wide-ranging vistas.*

## The Walk

Follow the village street past Bridegate Lane, and the Long Clawson road on your left, and take a footpath, waymarked to Hickling Pastures, between the houses on your right. Follow the footpath over the fields, using the plastic waymark arrows as your guide. A faintly defined path over the pastures initially keeps to the right hand slope of the hill, but soon bears left to reach a stile on the ridge.

Cross the stile and follow the ridge, keeping to the left of the hedge and passing to the left of the trig point. The summit is a little way off the public footpath and, although access is possible via a couple of gates, this is private land – and, in fact, the difference in altitude between the summit and the footpath is so slight as not significantly to affect the view.

Continuing along the ridge, cross a stile and find yourself on the right of the hedge. Ignore a track bearing right and keep to the right of the hedge, dropping down to a stile in the extreme corner of the field. Keep on over the fields, still on the right of the hedge, until you cross a thicket (passing a pond), after which you cross the corner of

114

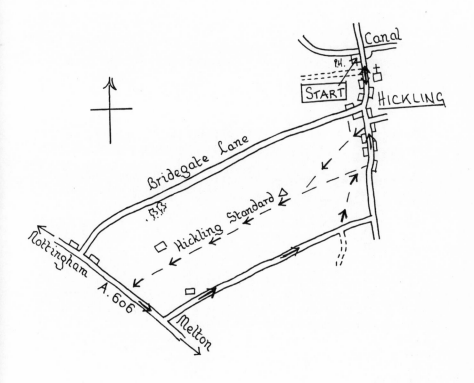

the next field to reach a stile close to the right hand corner. Pass through to the next big field, turn left and follow the hedge down to the A606 road.

Turn left along the road, keeping for safety's sake to the wide grass verge, and take the next turning on the left. A pleasant easy stroll follows along a quiet country lane. The way descends, gently at first and then more steeply as the view ahead opens out to offer a glorious view over the Vale of Belvoir and round towards Upper Broughton. Take your time – and take advantage of the wayside seat here to enjoy the scene.

Continue on along the road. I am no enthusiast for road walking, but this road is something else. Quiet, very rural, and with those splendid views. Pass a barn on the left, opposite a narrow lane, which leads to Upper Broughton. Just past the barn, take a footpath on the left, crossing a tricky little plank-bridge and stile. Continue over three fields, with the hedge on your left. Take particular note of the ridge and furrow pattern of the fields here. This is not so common these days, when modern farm practices have tended to eliminate the ancient corrugations, caused by the old style of plough, which travelled from end to end of the fields alternately in either direction, but always turning the earth to the same side and so forming the distinctive ridges.

In the fourth field, bear right, passing a pond and cross a stile part way over the field. Bear left down the next field to reach a gate in the far corner and join a lane. Follow the lane to a kissing-gate and the village road. Turn left through the village and back to the inn, to enjoy the wildlife – swans, ducks and coot – in the canal basin.

# 29 Wysall
## The Plough

The Plough is a typical old-fashioned village pub, occupying an elevated position at the northern end of this charming old village. The setting and the exterior layout, with picnic tables and hanging baskets in summer in the spacious garden area, add a unique touch of character. The interior is equally pleasing, with low-beamed ceilings, horse brasses and attractive bow windows. A friendly welcome is guaranteed.

This is a freehouse, offering Bass Pedigree to the beer drinkers, and Dry Black to the cider-holics. Full meals as well as bar snacks are available every lunchtime, except Sunday, between 12 noon and 2.15 pm. A speciality here is Grandma Batty's Yorkshire puddings, with a variety of savoury fillings – filling being the operative word, as I was obliged to call it quits without finishing my chicken supreme! They also do roast potatoes, again with a choice of fillings, and a selection of salads and cobs.

The beer garden provides a pleasant environment for children, dogs, lovers of fresh air and all those who, having purchased drinks (and had the courtesy to ask permission), choose to eat their own food here outside catering hours.

Telephone: Loughborough (0509) 880339.

*How to get there:* The pretty village of Wysall lies to the east of the A60 Nottingham to Loughborough road and is best approached, if coming from Nottingham, via Bradmore, or by way of Costock, if arriving from Loughborough. The Plough is on the Keyworth road, at the north end of the village.

*Parking:* The Plough has its own car park on the opposite side of the road, and patrons are welcome to leave their vehicles here for the duration of the walk.

*Public transport:* Wysall is served by Barton's Nottingham to Leicester bus service.

*Length of the walk:* 3½ miles. Maps: OS Landranger series 129 Nottingham and Loughborough, Pathfinder series SK 42/52 Loughborough North and Castle Donington, and SK 62/72 Scalford and Nether Broughton (GR 605274).

*Not so many years ago, one of the surest signs of spring was the sight of cyclists coasting down Wilford Hill with great bunches of bluebells strapped to their rear carriers, the harvest of a visit to Bunny Woods. Wiser counsel prevails today, and the bluebells are left to display their glory in its proper environment – the incomparable woodlands between Bunny and Wysall.*

## The Walk
Leave Wysall by the Keyworth road, taking the first turning to follow Bunny Lane, climbing steadily but easily for a good ½ mile. At the top of the hill, as the road bends leftward, pause to enjoy a splendid panoramic view over Nottingham and the Trent Valley. This view's days may well be numbered, because a new wood has been planted on the hillside here which will surely obscure the view when fully mature. But that will not be for some time yet.

Continue down the hill, taking care to avoid approaching traffic on the second bend. The road descends by a sunken way with woodland on either hand. At the end of the woods to the left, leave the road to join a bridleway (waymarked) following a clear route just inside the wood. There is a good view over the fields from here to Bunny village, with its prominent church spire – and the equally prominent tower of Bunny Hall. Also visible, in the distance, is the ubiquitous Ratcliffe on Soar Power Station.

On reaching a crossways, where the Wysall to Bunny footpath crosses, turn left over the stile (or through the adjacent snicket) and follow the waymarked route, sometime footpath and sometime wider track, as it winds, and then climbs steeply through the woods to

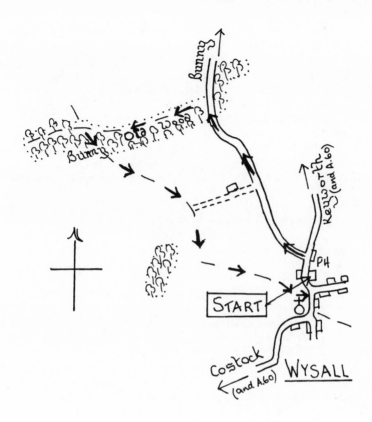

emerge eventually on the open hilltop. A prominent notice board here reminds us that this is Bunny Old Wood, a nature reserve under the care of the Nottinghamshire Wildlife Trust.

Go over the stile and enter a large field. The correct route from here crosses this vast prairie diagonally and, if the path is clear, this is the way you must go. If there is a growing crop in the field, however, the correct line of the path may not be evident, and you may choose to follow others around the field – bearing in mind first, that it is a long way, and second, that you are thereby trespassing. But then again, if you cross the field on the wrong line, you will also be trespassing! If going round the field, you first follow the edge of the wood, then a tall hedge, and finally a fence, to arrive at a plank bridge and a stile.

The next field is much smaller, and you should have no difficulty in finding your way across this one, to reach the exit stile in the far right hand corner, a perfect waymark over this field being the spire of

119

Wysall church.

Cross the stile and follow the waymarked path straight ahead, beside the fence and the ensuing hedge. Near the end of the second field, turn left over a plank bridge and follow the hedge straight ahead over one field. In the second field, after following the left of the hedge for a short distance, cross back to the right via a stile and continue on the right of the hedge over this and the next field.

Cross a stile in the extreme corner of this field and go over the next field, corner to corner, again with the church as your waymark. Cross a stile by the field gate and turn left, following the enclosed path to the road. Turn left, back to the inn.

# 30 Zouch
## The Rose and Crown

The Rose and Crown is an attractive country inn and restaurant on the banks of the Zouch Cut – a stretch of canal – right on the Leicestershire county boundary. The situation could scarcely be more agreeable, with the constant passage to and fro of pleasure boats on the cut, and a wealth of delightful walks beside the lovely river Soar and around the neighbouring villages.

The facilities at the inn consist of a single large room, one end being a traditional bar (with an incredibly vast working area) with the remainder of the accommodation given over to the restaurant facility. It is an old house, being certainly here well over a century ago when it was the Bull's Head, and very popular with the boatmen on the river Soar and the Zouch Cut. It retains its popularity today with, among others, the modern generation of leisure boaters. Sandwiched between the main road and the cut, there is not a lot of room to play with, but what there is, is used well. And if you choose your table wisely, you can enjoy the passing canal traffic as you dine. This is a pleasant country pub, with a variety of items decorating the inevitable oak beams: drip mats, china plates and a yoke (as of milk pails). The furnishings are tasteful, the atmosphere quiet and relaxing, and the service pleasant and courteous. Accommodation is available.

The Rose and Crown is a freehouse, and ales on offer include Theakston XB and Old Peculier, amongst others. Taunton's Draught Cider is likewise available. A full à la carte menu is available lunchtimes and evenings, not to mention traditional Sunday lunches and midday specials.

Overlooking the canal there is a garden area where well behaved dogs are welcome, and customers may eat their own picnics, when food is not otherwise available.

Telephone: Loughborough (0509) 842240.

*How to get there:* The tiny settlement of Zouch is situated on the A6006 Rempstone to Ashby road, just inside the Nottinghamshire county boundary, on the eastern side of the river Soar. It is best approached either from the A60 via Rempstone, or from the A6 trunk road via Hathern.

*Parking:* Parking is limited on the forecourt of the inn and, although the licensee does not object to customers parking here for the duration of their walk, reasonable folk will not mind using the public car park, ¼ mile or so up the road.

*Public transport:* Barton's Nottingham to Loughborough service calls at Zouch.

*Length of the walk:* 5½ miles (but the route can easily make two shorter walks). Maps: OS Landranger series 129 Nottingham and Loughborough, Pathfinder series SK 42/52 Loughborough North and Castle Donington (GR 508235).

*Zouch's attraction is undeniable, with its old mill, now converted to flats, the twin waterways of river and canal with their colourful craft plying to and fro – not to mention the inn itself. But it is the peaceful riverside meadows, perhaps, which most commend this walk. These, and the beautiful unspoilt villages of Sutton Bonington and Normanton on Soar through which we pass while on our journey.*

*This is an 'options' walk. The full distance is 5½ miles. But if you think this too far, there is no problem in opting for a shorter route. The Normanton section is 2¼ miles and the Devil's Elbow leg is 3¼ miles.*

## The Walk

*For the Normanton section,* follow the Rempstone road out of Zouch, and leave immediately by a waymarked footpath on the right, by a farm. Cross this first field to pass through a farm gate. The exit from the second field is to the right of the field gate, a combined stile and foot-

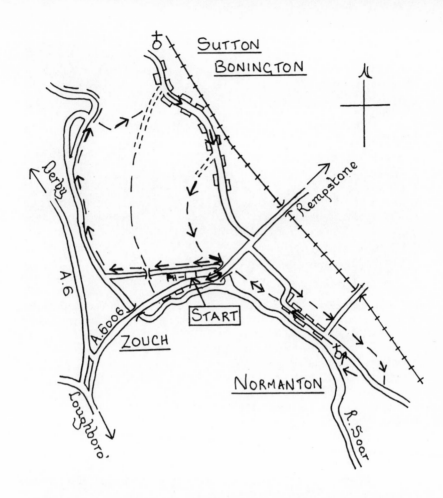

bridge between it and the field corner. Cross the third field, following the same general direction and emerge, via a stile, on a bend in the road at the beginning of Normanton village. Turn left here.

On reaching a second bend turn right, following the waymarked footpath. A delightful path ensues, over a series of grass fields behind the houses of the village, interconnected by easy stiles and footbridges.

Cross a road and continue, still beside fields, some of which are in arable use. The path crosses first to the right and then back to the left of the hedge, before crossing an open field and a dike. Bear right across the next field, making for a point to the right of an electricity

123

pylon, to reach the road. Turn right to follow the road back towards Normanton.

Leave the road again on the bend, by a footpath, left. Cross a stream by a footbridge and continue, heading towards the church. Signs of a path may be conspicuous by their absence, but keep right on and you will find that you arrive at a stile in the far corner of the field, beside a group of chalets. Cross the stile and bear left towards the river. Pass to the right of a red notice board, cross a stile and pass through a private garden, to arrive in the church grounds. A bench here is a super place to stop for a while and enjoy the life of the river.

Follow the church path to the road and turn left through the village. On reaching the bend at the top end of the village, rejoin the field path and return to Zouch by your outward route.

*For the Devil's Elbow section*, join the canal towpath at the bridge, just to the east of the inn. This is just a short length of canal – the Zouch Cut – provided specifically for the purpose of bypassing a weir, a natural obstruction to the navigability of the river Soar. The cut is often busy, with narrow boats and cruisers bustling to and fro, and you may be able to see the lock put through its paces.

Just beyond the lock the river is joined. Follow the riverside path for about a mile, for most of the way through gentle riverside meadows. It is an enjoyable walk, enlivened by the presence of waterfowl, passing pleasure boats, and an angler or two. The Soar is subject to flooding after heavy rain, and you have the choice of following either the riverside way or the top of the floodbank. Later, the path is flanked on the landward side by a low concrete wall, at just the right height to provide a welcome resting place.

Beyond Devil's Elbow – where the river has been diverted to bypass a severe bend, thus creating an island – a footpath will be seen leading off right. Climb over the floodwall here and cross a footbridge and stile and enter a field. Follow the hedge up the left of the field, turning left towards the end of the field to cross a stile beside a field gate and then a bridge. Continue straight ahead over the next field, ignoring a track which leads right to a farm gate. Aim for the extreme right hand corner of the field, where you will find a stile leading out into Pasture Lane. Look out for a tricky piece of masonry underfoot, as you emerge onto the lane. Turn left and continue into Sutton Bonington.

This was originally two villages – Sutton and Bonington – and is a charming place, with a number of fine old red-brick houses. It is also something of a special place in the agricultural world, for the University of Nottingham School of Agriculture is here, and the Ministry of Agriculture has an animal health facility in the village.

Follow the road south for ½ mile, leaving by a waymarked lane on the right, near a bus shelter. Bear left to cross a stile beside a field gate and follow the hedge on your left. In the second field, turn left through a gap in the hedge and cross the next field, corner to corner. Through the field gate keep straight on, bearing left to the angle of the hedge. Cross a stile and then turn right, following the hedge through to the road at Zouch.

# Bus Services

Barton Travel, Broad Marsh Bus Station, Nottingham
Nottingham (0602) 580070

East Midland Motor Services Limited, New Street, Chesterfield,
Derbyshire
Chesterfield (0246) 211007

Kettlewell (Retford) Limited, Grove Street, Retford, Notts DN22 6AI
Retford (0777) 860360

Lincolnshire Road Car Co Ltd, PO Box 15, St Marks Street, Lincoln
LN5 7BB
Lincoln (0522) 532424

Mansfield District Bus Company (As East Midland Motor Services
Limited)

Nottingham City Transport Limited, Lower Parliament Street,
Nottingham NG1 1GG
Nottingham (0602) 503665

Notts County Council Bus Line (information service only)
Nottingham (0602) 240000

Pathfinder (Newark) Limited, 17 High Street, Collingham, Newark,
Notts NG23 7LA
Newark (0636) 611885

Retford and District (Chesterfield) Limited, Church Street, Bawtry,
Doncaster, S Yorks
Doncaster (0302) 711729

South Notts Bus Company (As Nottingham City Transport)
Nottingham (0602) 503665

Trent Buses, Uttoxeter New Road, Derby
Derby (0332) 292200

Wrights of Newark (Travel Wright), Lincoln Road Garage, Newark on
Trent, Notts NG24 2DR
Newark (0636) 703813

# The Country Code

Enjoy the countryside and respect its life and work
Guard against all risk of fire
Fasten all gates
Keep your dogs under close control
Keep to public paths across farmland
Use gates and stiles to cross fences, hedges and walls
Leave livestock, crops and machinery alone
Take your litter home
Help to keep all water clean
Protect wild life, plants and trees
Take special care on country roads
Make no unnecessary noise